This booklet may be obtained from the

U.S. Fish and Wildlife Service
Division of Bird Habitat Conservation
4401 N. Fairfax Drive, Suite 110
Arlington, Virginia 22203
Phone (703) 358-1784

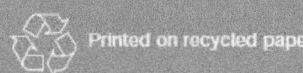

Printed on recycled paper.

North American Bird Conservation Initiative

Bird Conservation Region Descriptions

A Supplement to the
North American Bird Conservation Initiative
Bird Conservation Regions Map

U.S. NABCI Committee
September 2000

This booklet is a supplement to the North American Bird Conservation Initiative Bird Conservation Regions map. Both are available through the

U.S. Fish and Wildlife Service
Division of Bird Habitat Conservation
4401 N. Fairfax Drive, Suite 110
Arlington, Virginia 22203
Phone: (703) 358-1784

Acknowledgments

The U.S. NABCI Committee wishes to express its appreciation to the Canadian and Mexican NABCI Committees for preparing descriptions of their countries' Bird Conservation Regions (BCRs) and for delineating the Canadian and Mexican BCRs seen on the North American Bird Conservation Initiative Bird Conservation Regions Map.

Photo Credits

Photos from top to bottom: Royal Terns, Stephen C. Delaney, U.S. Environmental Protection Agency; Long-billed Dowitcher, Karen Hollingsworth; Lichtenstein's Oriole, James C. Leopold; Hooded Mergansers, Karen Hollingsworth.

North American Bird Conservation Initiative

Bird Conservation Region Descriptions

A Supplement to the
North American Bird Conservation Initiative
Bird Conservation Regions Map

U.S. NABCI Committee
September 2000

Contents

Introduction

The North American Bird Conservation Initiative

The purpose of the North American Bird Conservation Initiative (NABCI) is to ensure the long-term health of North America's native bird populations by increasing the effectiveness of existing and new bird conservation initiatives, enhancing coordination among the initiatives, and fostering greater cooperation among the continent's three national governments and their people. All of this will be done with appreciation of the cultural and biological differences that make each country unique.

This conservation approach is expressed through NABCI's goal of delivering the full spectrum of bird conservation through regionally based, biologically driven, landscape-oriented partnerships. "Regionally based" partnerships involve all stakeholders across ecoregions and are the proven means of effectively delivering bird conservation. "Biologically driven" means that there must be explicit linkages among population objectives, habitat goals, and conservation actions. It also means that evaluation and adaptability are critical components of successful conservation efforts. "Landscape-oriented" recognizes the response of bird populations to habitat conditions across broad ecoregions and the need for conservation to operate at multiple geographic scales.

The NABCI vision is one of habitat partnerships, based upon the North American Waterfowl Management Plan's joint venture model, covering the continent coast-to-coast. It is hoped that each existing and new partnership will consider delivering conservation of all birds in all habitats and that these partnerships eventually move toward conservation of biological diversity using Bird Conservation Regions (BCRs) as the ecological unit in which to achieve their goals.

The Development of Bird Conservation Regions

A mapping team comprised of members from the United States, Mexico, and Canada assembled at the first international NABCI workshop held in Puebla, Mexico, in November 1998, to develop a consistent spatial framework for bird conservation for North America. After agreeing on general principles, they adopted a hierarchical framework of nested ecological units delineated by the Commission for Environmental Cooperation.

The team's U.S. members met in December of that year in Memphis, Tennessee, to apply the framework to the United States and develop a proposed map of BCRs. The map and its BCR descriptions, along with an explanation of the ecological framework and philosophy behind their development, was published in *A Proposed Framework for Delineating Ecologically-based Planning, Implementation, and Evaluation Units for Cooperative Bird Conservation in the U.S.* This document was widely distributed for review in March 1999. Shortly after the comment period closed in October, the team evaluated the comments received and produced a revised map. The map was presented to and approved by the U.S. NABCI Committee during its November 1, 1999, meeting.

The Canadian mapping team conducted broad consultations on the preliminary boundaries that emerged from the Puebla meeting. With some modifications, the boundaries in Canada were accepted by the bird conservation community for a 3-year trial period. The Canadian and U.S. mapping teams subsequently worked together to develop consistent BCR lines for the two countries.

The descriptions for BCRs partly or wholly in Mexico also include information about Important Bird Areas (IBAs), where this program has become the central organizing theme for work under NABCI. The development of BCR boundaries was undertaken by the Mexican NABCI Coordinator and with support from Conabio's Department of Geographic Information Systems. Boundaries and descriptions were defined using a combination of references: Commission for Environmental Cooperation Level I and Level II Ecoregion Maps (Commission for Environmental Cooperation. 1997.), distributional bird maps (Escalante, P., A. Navarro, and T. Peterson. 1993.), and *Areas de Importancia para la Conservación de las Aves en México* (Arizmendi, M.C., and L. Márques–Valdelamar, editors. 2000.). Because conservation efforts within Mexican BCRs will focus on these IBAs, they are included on the North American Bird Conservation Initiative Bird Conservation Regions map.

The map is a dynamic tool. Its BCR boundaries will change over time as new scientific information becomes available. It is expected that the map will be updated every three years, with the next update occurring in November 2002.

Bird Conservation Region Descriptions

1. Aleutian/Bering Sea Islands

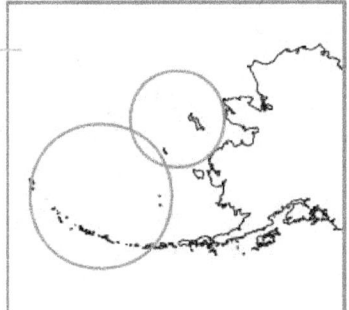

Included in this region are the Aleutian Islands, extending west-ward from the Alaskan mainland for 1,100 miles, and the Bering Sea islands, including the Pribilofs, St. Matthew, Hall, St. Lawrence, and Little Diomede. The Aleutian chain is volcanic in origin, with a maritime climate in which wind is ever present. Vegetation at higher elevations consists of dwarf shrub communities, mainly willow and crowberry. Meadows and marshes of herbs, sedges, and grasses are plentiful, and some islands have ericaceous bogs. Sea ice does not extend to the Aleutians and permafrost is generally absent; however, sea ice is an important feature of the Bering Sea. Seabirds are a dominant component of this region's avifauna, and several species, including the Red-legged Kittiwake, Least Auklet, and Whiskered Auklet, breed only in this region. Southern Hemisphere procellariiforms occur regularly in the offshore waters of the southern Bering Sea and northern Gulf of Alaska during Alaskan summers. The breeding diversity of passerines (mainly Lapland Longspur, Snow Bunting, and Gray-crowned Rosy-Finch), and shorebirds (including Black Oystercatcher, Dunlin, Ruddy Turnstone, and Rock Sandpiper) is low. However, McKay's Bunting, the only endemic Alaskan passerine, is restricted to this area.

2. Western Alaska

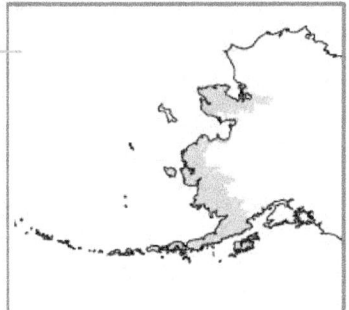

This region consists of the Subarctic Coastal Plain of western Alaska and the Alaska Peninsula Mountains. Wet and mesic graminoid herbaceous communities dominate the lowlands, and numerous ponds, lakes, and rivers dot the landscape. Tall shrub communities are found along rivers and streams, and low shrub communities occupy uplands. Forests of spruce and hardwoods penetrate the region on the eastern edge. Permafrost is continuous, except in southern parts of the region. High densities of breeding waterfowl and shorebirds are found on the coastal plain of the Yukon and Kuskokwim Rivers. Intertidal areas here and lagoons of the northern side of the Alaska Peninsula support millions of shorebirds during migration, including Dunlin, Western Sandpiper, Red Knot, and Bar-tailed Godwit. The coast of the Alaska Peninsula supports high concentrations of wintering sea ducks, including Steller's Eider, Harlequin, Oldsquaw, Surf Scoter, and Black Scoter. Passerine diversity is greatest in tall, riparian shrub habitats, where Arctic Warbler, Gray-cheeked Thrush, and Blackpoll Warbler nest. Gyrfalcon and Rough-legged Hawk nest along the riverine cliffs. Mainland sea cliffs are occupied by nesting colonies of Black-legged Kittiwake, Common Murre, and Pelagic Cormorant.

3. Arctic Plains and Mountains

This region includes low-lying, coastal tundra and drier uplands of the Arctic mountains across the entire northern edge of North America. Because of thick and continuous permafrost, surface water dominates the landscape (20–50 percent of the coastal plain). Freezing and thawing form a patterned mosaic of polygonal ridges and ponds, and many rivers bisect the plain and flow into the Arctic Ocean. The ocean surface is generally frozen 9 to 10 months of the year, and the ice pack is never far from shore. Because of the wetness, waterfowl and shorebirds dominate the avian community and passerines are scarce. The most abundant breeding birds on the coastal plain include Northern Pintail, King Eider, Oldsquaw, American Golden-Plover, Semipalmated Sandpiper, Pectoral Sandpiper, Red-necked Phalarope, and Lapland Longspur. Several Old World species, including the Arctic Warbler and Bluethroat, penetrate the region from the west. Taiga passerines, such as Gray-cheeked Thrush and Yellow Warbler, reach the region along drainage systems, and raptors, including Gyrfalcon and Rough-legged Hawk, nest commonly along major rivers. Few bird species winter in the region.

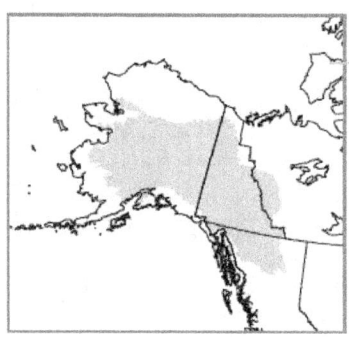

4. Northwestern Interior Forest

The interplay of elevation, permafrost, surface water, fire, and aspect creates an extensive patchwork of ecological types. Forest habitat in the region is dominated by white spruce, black spruce, poplars, and paper birch. Tall shrub communities occur along rivers, drainages, and near treeline. Bogs, consisting of low shrubs and shrub-graminoid communities, are common in the lowlands. Alpine dwarf scrub communities are common throughout mountainous regions, and the highest elevations are generally devoid of vegetation. Lowlands, bottomlands, and flats harbor many species of migrating and breeding ducks (e.g., Northern Pintail, Northern Shoveler, Green-winged Teal) and swans. These and the forested lowlands and uplands support breeding shorebirds, such as Greater and Lesser Yellowlegs; Purple, White-rumped, Buff-breasted, Solitary, and Spotted Sandpipers; Sanderling; and Common Snipe. American Golden-Plovers and Surfbirds are found in alpine habitats in mountainous ecoregions. Western Sandpiper, Long-billed Dowitcher, Short-billed Dowitcher, Hudsonian Godwit, and Dunlin use stopover sites along the coast that are also primary wintering habitat for Rock Sandpipers. The suite of passerines inhabiting upland communities in the region includes Boreal Chickadee; Swainson's and Gray-cheeked Thrush; American Pipit; White-crowned, American Tree, Harris', and Fox Sparrows; Snow Bunting; and Common Redpoll. At high elevations, Horned Lark and Lapland Longspur are common breeders.

5. Northern Pacific Rainforest

The coastal rainforest stretches from the western Gulf of Alaska south through British Columbia and the Pacific Northwest to northern California. Its maritime climate is characterized by heavy precipitation and mild temperatures. The region is dominated by forests of western hemlock and Sitka spruce in the far north, with balsam fir, Douglas fir, and coast redwood becoming more important farther south. Broadleaf forests are found along large mainland river drainages. High priority breeding forest birds include the Spotted Owl, Marbled Murrelet, Northern Goshawk, Chestnut-backed Chickadee, Red-breasted Sapsucker, and Hermit Warbler. The coast of the Northern Pacific Rainforest is characterized by river deltas and pockets of estuarine and freshwater wetlands set within steep, rocky shorelines. These wetlands provide critical breeding, wintering, and migration habitat for internationally significant populations of waterfowl and other wetland-dependent species. The area includes major stopover sites for migrating shorebirds, especially Western Sandpipers and Dunlins. Black Oystercatchers, Rock Sandpipers, Black Turnstones, and Surfbirds are common wintering species. Nearshore marine areas support many breeding and wintering sea ducks. Many seabirds breed on offshore islands, including important populations of Ancient Murrelet, Rhinoceros Auklet, Tufted Puffin, Common Murre, Western and Glaucous-winged Gull, and Leach's Storm-Petrel. Pelagic waters provide habitat for large numbers of shearwaters, storm-petrels, alcids, and Black-footed Albatross.

6. Boreal Taiga Plains

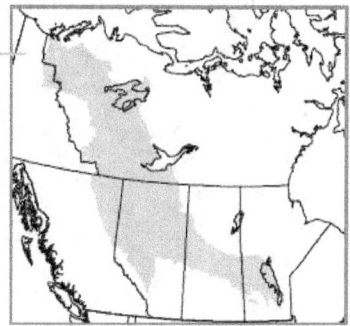

The Boreal Taiga Plains region is dominated by the Mackenzie River and its tributaries in its northern portion and the boreal transition zone in the south. Black spruce is a dominant species in the open, coniferous forests of the north, while the warmer better-drained southerly locales support mixed-wood forests of white and black spruce, lodgepole pine, tamarack, white birch, trembling aspen, and balsam poplar. Low-lying wetlands cover 25–50 percent of the zone, and patterned ground features are common. A large portion of the area is underlain by permafrost, creating a landscape that is seasonally waterlogged over large areas. Important birds of the region include Whooping Crane, American White Pelican, Marsh Wren, Wilson's Phalarope, Yellow-headed Blackbird, Sharp-tailed Grouse, Mountain Bluebird, Great Gray Owl, Swainson's Hawk, and Fox Sparrow. The Mackenzie Valley forms one of North America's most traveled migratory corridors for waterfowl breeding along the Arctic Coast.

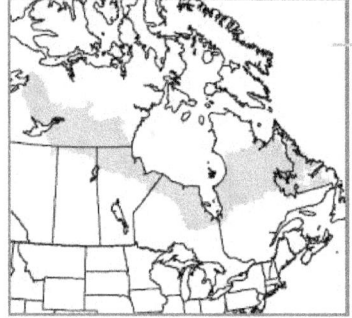

7. Taiga Shield and Hudson Plains

This BCR includes the Hudson Plains—the largest extensive area of wetlands in the world—and extends east and west onto the Canadian Shield. The subarctic climate is characterized by relatively short, cool summers with prolonged periods of daylight and long, very cold winters. The poorly drained areas of the Hudson Plains support dense sedge-moss-lichen covers, with open woodlands of black spruce and tamarack in better-drained sites. Coastal marshes and extensive tidal flats are present along the coastline. The Canadian Shield is characterized in upland sites and along rivers by open, mixed-wood forests of white spruce, balsam fir, trembling aspen, balsam poplar, and white birch. Further north, approaching the limit of tree growth, stunted black spruce and jack pine dominate, accompanied by alder, willow, and tamarack in the fens and bogs. Thousands of lakes and wetlands occur in glacially carved depressions, and peat-covered lowlands are commonly waterlogged or wet for prolonged periods due to discontinuous but widespread permafrost. The abundance of water provides an important habitat for breeding waterfowl. Representative birds include Black Scoter, Whimbrel, Rock and Willow Ptarmigan, Gray-cheeked Thrush, American Tree Sparrow, Short-billed Dowitcher, Common Redpoll, Harris' Sparrow, Northern Shrike, Blackpoll Warbler, Fox Sparrow, and Rough-legged Hawk. The coasts of Hudson and James Bay provide critical shorebird staging habitat, funneling millions of birds southwards during fall migration.

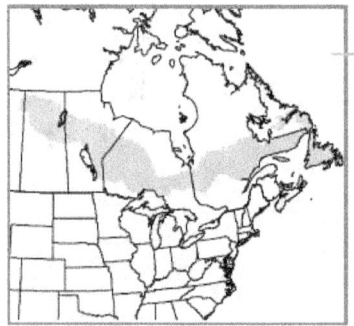

8. Boreal Softwood Shield

The Boreal Softwood Shield is a broad, U-shaped region comprised of seacoasts in the east and vast areas that are more than 80 percent forested by closed stands of conifers, largely white and black spruce, balsam fir, and tamarack. Toward the south, broadleaf trees, such as white birch, trembling aspen, and balsam poplar are more widely distributed, as are white, red, and jack pine. The region is a broadly rolling mosaic of uplands and associated wetlands, dotted with numerous small to medium-sized lakes. Peatlands are common in wetland areas. Representative birds include American Black Duck, Purple Sandpiper, Yellow Rail, Yellow-bellied Flycatcher, Black-backed Woodpecker, Boreal Owl, and Mourning, Palm, Bay-breasted, Connecticut, Cape May, Magnolia, and Tennessee Warblers. Coastlines and offshore areas in the east are important year-round for breeding and wintering seabirds.

9. Great Basin

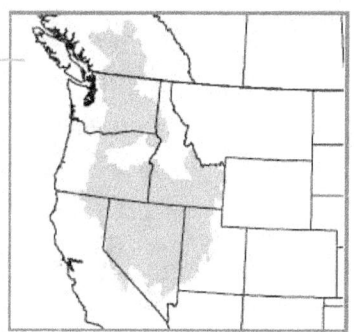

This large and complex region includes the Northern Basin and Range, Columbia Plateau, and the eastern slope of the Cascade Range. This area is dry due to its position in the rainshadow of the Cascade Range and the Sierra Nevada. Grasslands, sagebrush, and other xeric shrubs dominate the flats and lowlands, with piñon-juniper woodlands and open ponderosa pine forests on higher slopes. Lodgepole pine/sub-alpine fir forests occur at higher elevations on north-facing slopes. Several substantial lowland wetlands are extremely important to shorebirds, including breeding American Avocet; Black-necked Stilt; and Willet, migrating Wilson's Phalarope, and other water birds, notably Eared Grebe. The region is also important for breeding Mountain Plover and Snowy Plover. Most of North American breeding White-faced Ibis and California Gulls nest in marshes and lakes scattered across the region. The Great Salt Lake and adjacent marshes host large numbers of American White Pelican, Cinnamon Teal, Northern Pintail, Redhead, Tundra Swan, and other waterfowl and many species of migrant shorebirds. Sage Grouse, Sage Sparrow, Sage Thrasher, and Brewer's Sparrow are priority land birds of lowlands, with White-headed Woodpecker, Flammulated Owl, and Cassin's Finch leading the list of characteristic birds of the region's pine forests.

10. Northern Rockies

Included in this area are the Northern Rocky Mountains and outlying ranges in both the United States and Canada, and also the intermontane Wyoming Basin and Fraser Basin. The Rockies are dominated by a variety of coniferous forest habitats. Drier areas are dominated by ponderosa pine, with Douglas fir and lodgepole pine at higher elevations and Engelman spruce and subalpine fir even higher. More mesic forests to the north and west are dominated by western larch, grand fir, western red cedar, and western hemlock. High priority forest birds include the Flammulated Owl, Lewis' and Black-backed Woodpecker, Olive-sided Flycatcher, Townsend's Warbler, Rufous Hummingbird, Black Swift, and Blue Grouse. Barrow's Goldeneye, Harlequin Duck, and Trumpeter Swan breed in high-elevation lakes and streams. The Wyoming Basin and other lower-lying valleys are characterized by sagebrush shrubland and shrubsteppe habitat, much of which has been degraded by conversion to other uses or invasion of non-native plants. High priority birds include Sage Grouse, Ferruginous Hawk, Brewer's Sparrow, and Sage Thrasher.

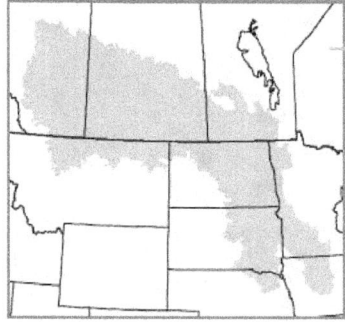

11. Prairie Potholes

The Prairie Pothole region is a glaciated area of mixed-grass prairie in the west and tallgrass prairie in the east. This is the most important waterfowl production area on the North American continent, despite extensive wetland drainage and tillage of native grasslands. Breeding dabbling duck density may exceed 100 pairs per square mile in some areas during years with favorable wetland conditions. The region comprises the core of the breeding range of most dabbling duck and several diving duck species, as well as providing critical breeding and migration habitat for over 200 other bird species, including such priority species as Franklin's Gull, Yellow Rail, and Piping Plover. Baird's Sparrow, Sprague's Pipit, Chestnut-collared Longspur, Wilson's Phalarope, Marbled Godwit, and American Avocet are among the many priority non-waterfowl species breeding in this region. Wetland areas also provide key spring migration sites for Hudsonian Godwit, American Golden-Plover, White-rumped Sandpiper, and Buff-breasted Sandpiper. Continued wetland degradation and fragmentation of remaining grasslands threaten future suitability of the Prairie Pothole region for all of these birds.

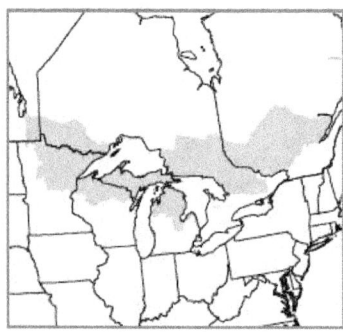

12. Boreal Hardwood Transition

This region is characterized by coniferous and northern hardwood forests, nutrient-poor soils, and numerous clear lakes, bogs, and river flowage. All of the world's Kirtland's Warblers breed here, as do the majority of Golden-winged Warblers and Connecticut Warblers. Other important forest birds include the Black-billed Cuckoo, Veery, and Rose-breasted Grosbeak. Great Lakes coastal estuaries, river flowage, large shallow lakes, and natural wild rice lakes are used by many breeding and migrating water birds. Yellow Rail are among the important wetland species, and islands in the Great Lakes support large colonies of Caspian and Common Terns. Although breeding ducks are sparsely distributed, stable water conditions allow for consistent reproductive success. Wood Duck, Mallard, American Black Duck, Ring-necked Duck, and Common Goldeneye are common breeding species in this region. Threats to wetland habitat in this region include recreational development, cranberry operations, peat harvesting, and drainage.

13. Lower Great Lakes/St. Lawrence Plain

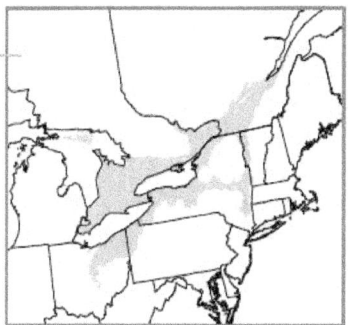

The Lower Great Lakes/St. Lawrence Plain covers the low-lying areas to the south of the Canadian Shield and north of various highland systems in the United States. In addition to important lakeshore habitats and associated wetlands, this region was originally covered with a mixture of oak-hickory, northern hardwood, and mixed-coniferous forests. Very little of the forests remains today due primarily to agricultural conversion. The highest priority bird in remnant forests is the Cerulean Warbler. Because of agriculture, this is now the largest and most important area of grassland in the Northeast, providing habitat for such species as Henslow's Sparrow and Bobolink. Agricultural abandonment may temporarily favor shrub-nesting species, such as Golden-winged Warbler and American Woodcock, but increasingly, agricultural land is being lost to urbanization. This physiographic area also is extremely important to stopover migrants, attracting some of the largest concentrations of migrant passerines, hawks, shorebirds, and waterbirds in eastern North America. Much of these concentrations occurs along threatened lakeshore habitats.

14. Atlantic Northern Forest

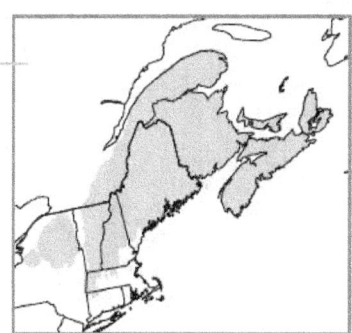

The nutrient-poor soils of northernmost New England and the Adirondack Mountains support spruce-fir forests on more northerly and higher sites and northern hardwoods elsewhere. Virtually all of the world's Bicknell's Thrush breed on mountaintops in this region. Other important forest birds include the Canada Warbler and Bay-breasted Warbler. Coastal wetlands are inhabited by Nelson's Sharp-tailed Sparrow; rocky intertidal areas are important for wintering Purple Sandpipers; and muddy intertidal habitats are critical as Semipalmated Sandpiper staging sites. Common Eiders and Black Guillemots breed in coastal habitats, while Leach's Storm-Petrels, gulls, terns, and the southernmost populations of many breeding alcids nest on offshore islands. Beaver ponds and shores of undisturbed lakes and ponds provide excellent waterfowl breeding habitat, particularly for American Black Duck, Hooded and Common Mergansers, and Common Goldeneye. The Hudson and Connecticut River valleys are important corridors for Brant, Green-winged Teal, and other waterfowl migrating from New England and Quebec. Because inland wetlands freeze, coastal wetlands are used extensively by dabbling ducks, sea ducks, and geese during winter and migration.

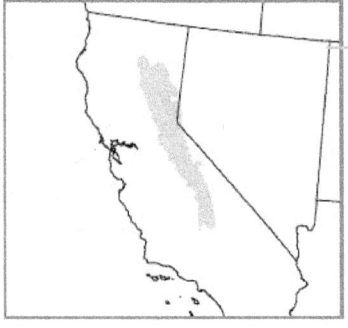

15. Sierra Nevada

The Sierra Nevada range rises sharply from the Great Basin on the east and slopes gently toward the Central Valley of California on the west. Vegetation at lower elevations is dominated by ponderosa pine on the west and lodgepole pine on the east, with fir, spruce, and alpine tundra at higher elevations. The area provides habitat for Hermit Warbler, White-headed Woodpecker, and Mountain Quail at higher elevations and Nuttall's Woodpecker, Oak Titmouse, and California Thrasher on the western slopes.

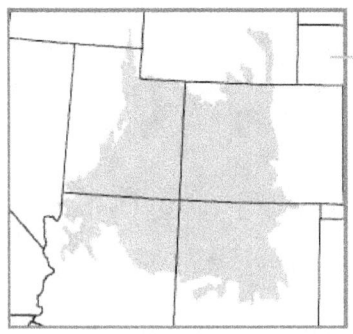

16. Southern Rockies/Colorado Plateau

This topographically complex region includes the Wasatch and Uinta Mountains to the west and the Southern Rocky Mountains to the east, separated by the rugged tableland of the Colorado Plateau. Various coniferous forest types (often lodgepole pine) interspersed with aspen dominate higher elevations. These are replaced by piñon-juniper woodlands on the lower plateaus. Important birds also segregate into elevational bands, with Brown-capped Rosy-Finch and White-tailed Ptarmigan in alpine tundra, Williamson's Sapsucker in conifers, Virginia's Warbler and Lewis' Woodpecker in montane shrub sites, and most of the world's breeding Gray Vireos in piñon-juniper. High arid plains and dry upland short-grass prairies provide critical breeding areas for Mountain Plover. San Luis Valley wetlands and surrounding uplands support one of the highest densities of nesting waterfowl in North America and provide migration habitat for Sandhill Cranes and other wetland species.

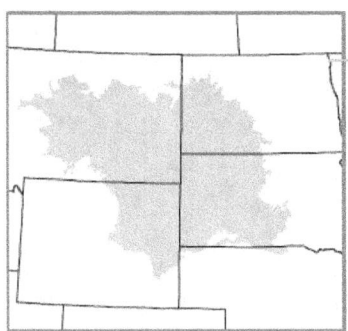

17. Badlands and Prairies

This semi-arid rolling plain is dominated by a mixed-grass prairie that lies west and south of the glaciated Prairie Pothole region, east of the Rocky Mountains, and north of the true shortgrass prairie. Due in large part to the continued dominance of ranching as a land use, many contiguous grassland tracts of significant size persist in this area. As a result, this area is habitat for some of the healthiest populations of high priority dry-grassland birds on the continent, including Mountain Plover, McCown's Longspur, and Long-billed Curlew. The relatively small number of wetlands in the region, including small impoundments created to serve as livestock water sources, receives intensive use by upland nesting waterfowl and broods.

18. Shortgrass Prairie

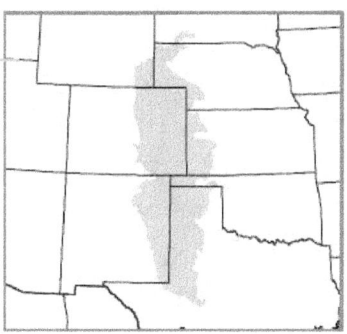

The Shortgrass Prairie lies in the rainshadow of the Rocky Mountains, where arid conditions greatly limit the stature and diversity of vegetation. Some of the continent's highest priority birds breed in this area, including the Mountain Plover, McCown's Longspur, Long-billed Curlew, Ferruginous Hawk, Burrowing Owl, and Lesser Prairie-Chicken. Reasons for the precarious status of these birds are poorly understood but could involve a reduction in the diversity of grazing pressure as bison and prairie dogs have largely been replaced by cattle. For migrants, it is possible that conditions on wintering grounds could also be having a negative impact. Numerous rivers, such as the Platte, drain out of the Rocky Mountains through this region toward the Mississippi Valley. These rivers created broad, braided, and treeless wetlands that are heavily used by migrating waterfowl, shorebirds, and cranes. Hydrological simplification has resulted in the invasion of trees and shrubs that support breeding eastern riparian birds, but otherwise greatly reduce the value of the areas as wetlands. The Playa Lakes area in the southern portion of this region consists of numerous shallow wetlands that support many wintering ducks, migrant shorebirds, and some important breeding species, such as the Snowy Plover.

19. Central Mixed-grass Prairie

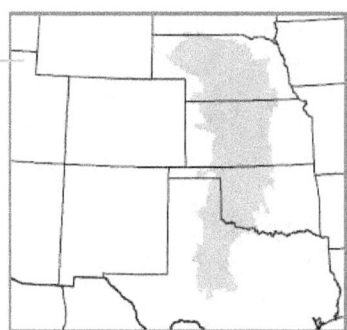

The Central Mixed-grass Prairie extends from the edge of shortgrass prairie on the west to the beginning of tallgrass prairie and savanna-like habitat to the east. There are vast areas in this region converted extensively to agriculture as well as extensive areas of remaining high-quality grassland in the Nebraska Sandhills and other sectors. The BCR includes some of the best remaining areas for Greater Prairie-Chicken and Henslow's Sparrow. Sandbars along the larger rivers host a large percentage of the continent's breeding Interior Least Terns. The region is an important spring migration area for American Avocet, Semipalmated Sandpiper, and Buff-breasted Sandpiper. Depressional wetlands concentrated in the Rainwater Basin and in playa lakes in the southern stretches of the area annually provide habitat for nearly 2 million ducks and 1 million geese. The mid-continent population of Northern Pintail and White-fronted Goose are particularly dependent on these wetland resources. However, wetland drainage and modification and sediment accumulation have jeopardized the integrity of these important landscape features.

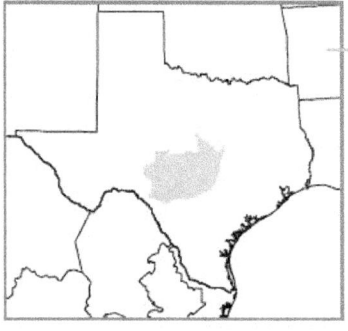

20. Edwards Plateau

This dissected Hill Country of central Texas is clearly demarcated on the east and south by a fault line and grades into the Chihuahuan Desert and Great Plains to the west and north. The native vegetation is a mesquite, juniper, and oak savanna that is the core of the breeding range of the endangered Black-capped Vireo and Golden-cheeked Warbler. Other priority breeding birds include the Scissor-tailed Flycatcher and Bell's Vireo. Intensive grazing by goats has caused vegetation to shift from grass to thicket dominance. Suburban expansion is a more recent threat to bird habitat in the Edwards Plateau.

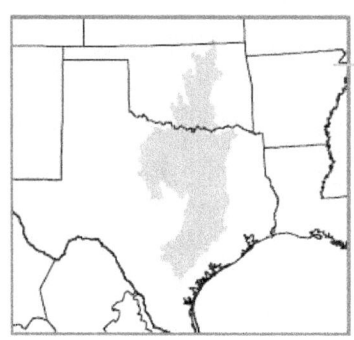

21. Oaks and Prairies

This transition zone between the Great Plains and the forests of the eastern United States is a complex mix of prairie, savanna, cross timbers, and shrubland. Among the priority landbirds that use this mix of woodland and open country are the Scissor-tailed Flycatcher, Painted Bunting, and Mississippi Kite, with a small population of Black-capped Vireos in areas of denser shrub. Agriculture and urbanization have made tremendous impacts on this region, leaving very little natural habitat available for healthy priority bird populations.

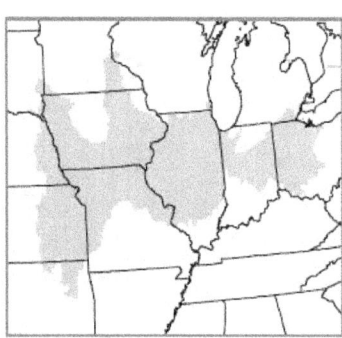

22. Eastern Tallgrass Prairie

This region includes what was formerly the tallest and lushest grasslands of the Great Plains. Beech-maple forest dominated in the eastern sections, and the prairie and woodland ecotone between the two was marked by a broad and dynamic oak-dominated savanna. The modern landscape of the Eastern Tallgrass Prairie is dominated by agriculture. Threats to the upland and wetland habitats of this region include urbanization, recreational development, and agricultural expansion. High priority grassland birds that persist in some areas include the Greater Prairie-Chicken and Henslow's Sparrow. Cerulean Warblers are in some wooded areas, and Red-headed Woodpecker leads the list of savanna specialists.

23. Prairie Hardwood Transition

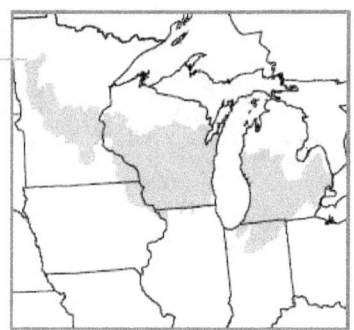

Prairies once dominated this region in the west and south and beech-maple forest in the north and east, separated by an oak savanna. There are still remnant populations of Greater Prairie-Chicken in grasslands and Cerulean Warbler and other forest-breeding migrants to the northeast. Early successional habitat is used by Golden-winged Warblers, Henslow's Sparrows, and American Woodcock. Glaciation has resulted in numerous pot-hole-type wetlands and shallow lakes, and the Great Lakes' coastal estuaries are the destinations of many rivers. Additional important waterfowl lakeshore-wetland habitats range from emergent marshes and diked impoundments to normally ice-free deepwater habitats valuable for diving ducks. This region is second only to the Prairie Pothole region in terms of support of high densities of breeding waterfowl, including Mallard, Blue-winged Teal, Wood Duck, and Redhead.

24. Central Hardwoods

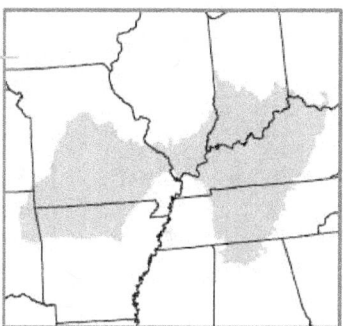

The Ozark Mountains on the west and Interior Low Plateaus on the east are geologically similar to each other but are bisected by the floodplain of the Mississippi River and its larger tributaries. The entire area is dominated by an oak-hickory deciduous forest inhabited by interior forest species, such as Cerulean Warbler, Worm-eating Warbler, and Louisiana Waterthrush. The region includes some of the most extensive forests in the middle of the continent and is probably a source for populations of these birds for many surrounding areas. Among early succession birds, this is the last major stronghold of the Eastern Bewick's Wren. Restoration of prairie, glade, and barren habitat is a conservation priority. Although Wood Ducks are the primary breeding waterfowl, the region holds more significance for waterfowl as a migratory staging area. The floodplains of the river systems exhibit a diversity of habitats (e.g., floodplain forests, emergent wetlands, and submerged aquatic beds), all of which are utilized by migrating waterfowl. Large concentrations of waterfowl, including Mallard, Lesser Scaup, and Canvasback, are common during both spring and fall migration. Threats to the habitats of the region include agricultural conversion of floodplain habitats and urbanization.

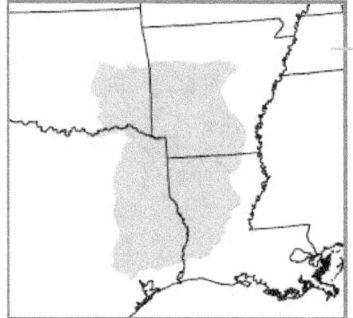

25. West Gulf Coastal Plain/Ouachitas

Pines dominate this area, largely shortleaf pine in the north, including the Ouachita Mountains, and longleaf pine in the south. This westernmost part of the eastern United States forest also includes hardwood-dominated bottomlands along the Arkansas River and other drainages. Red-cockaded Woodpecker is the highest priority bird in pine habitat, which is also inhabited by Bachman's Sparrow and Brown-headed Nuthatch. Conversion of the native pine forests to industrial loblolly plantations provides some bird habitat but is less useful for the highest priority species. The river and stream bottoms provide habitat used by Swainson's Warbler and large numbers of nesting herons and egrets. Bottomland hardwoods and associated wetlands support substantial wintering populations of a number of waterfowl species—principally Mallards, and breeding and wintering Wood Ducks—and are a primary migration corridor for significant numbers of other dabbling ducks. The primary threats to bottomland hardwood wetlands in the region are from reservoirs and timber harvest and subsequent conversion to pine plantation, pasture, or other land uses.

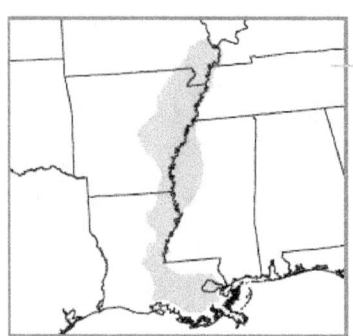

26. Mississippi Alluvial Valley

The Lower Mississippi Alluvial Valley consists of approximately 24 million acres of alluvial floodplain south of the Mississippi River's confluence with the Ohio River. Prior to European settlement, this was the greatest bottomland hardwood forest on earth and was subject to massive annual flood events of the Mississippi River and its tributaries. These forested wetlands were the main wintering area for mid-continent Mallards, Wood Ducks, and other waterfowl species. Flood control and deforestation for agriculture began more than 100 years ago. Today, less than 25 percent of the region remains forested, and flooding has been reduced by about 90 percent. Despite these changes, the region still winters large numbers of waterfowl, estimated at about 9 percent of the continental duck population. With the large reduction in native habitat and natural flooding, the major waterfowl management issue today is providing enough foraging habitat on managed private and public lands to reliably meet the needs of wintering ducks and geese. Many shorebird species also use managed wetlands for migration stopover sites. Remnant forests harbor populations of Swainson's Warbler, Prothonotary Warbler, and Swallow-tailed Kite. The region provides excellent colonial waterbird habitat, particularly to the south where large numbers of White Ibis, Yellow-crowned Night-Heron, and other herons and egrets nest.

27. Southeastern Coastal Plain

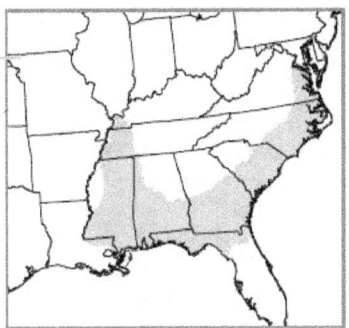

This region includes extensive riverine swamps and marsh complexes along the Atlantic Coast. Interior forest vegetation is dominated by longleaf, slash, and loblolly pine forests. Priority landbirds include the Red-cockaded Woodpecker, Painted Bunting, Bachman's Sparrow, Swainson's Warbler, and Swallow-Tailed Kite. Coastal intertidal habitats provide critical wintering areas for American Oystercatcher, important wintering and spring migration areas for Short-billed Dowitcher and Dunlin, and important fall staging areas for Red Knot. Sizable numbers of Brown Pelicans and various terns breed on offshore islands. Coastal areas provide important nesting and foraging habitats for large numbers of herons, egrets, ibis, terns, and other species. Coastal areas winter large numbers of Canvasback, Mallard, American Wigeon, Redhead, and the majority of the continent's population of Tundra Swans. Managed impoundments in coastal areas are important to migrating and wintering dabbling ducks, including American Black Duck.

28. Appalachian Mountains

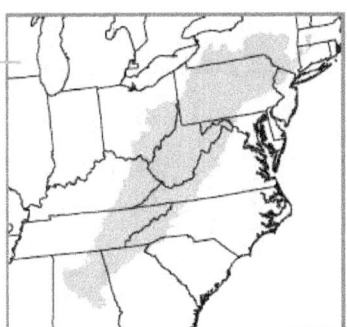

Included in this area are the Blue Ridge, the Ridge and Valley Region, the Cumberland Plateau, the Ohio Hills, and the Allegheny Plateau. The rugged terrain is generally dominated by oak-hickory and other deciduous forest types at lower elevations and by various combinations of pine, hemlock, spruce, and fir in higher areas. While flatter portions are in agricultural use, the majority of most segments of this region are forested. Priority forest birds include Cerulean Warbler at low elevations and Black-throated Blue Warbler at high elevations. Golden-winged Warblers are in early successional areas, and Henslow's Sparrows are in grasslands. While not as important for waterfowl as coastal regions, the Appalachian region contains the headwaters of several major eastern river systems that are used by various waterfowl species during migration. In addition, large wetland complexes, such as Canaan Valley in West Virginia, and isolated beaver-created wetlands provide habitat for Wood Duck breeding.

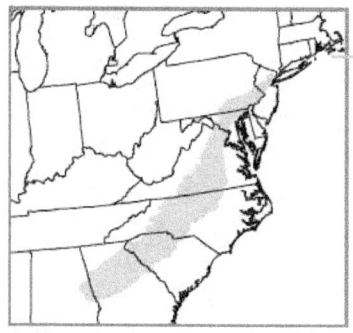

29. Piedmont

The Piedmont is transitional between the mountainous Appalachians and the flat coastal plain and is dominated by pine and mixed southern hardwoods. Priority landbirds include Red-cockaded Woodpecker, Bachman's Sparrow, and Brown-headed Nuthatch. Interior wetlands, reservoirs, and riverine systems provide migration and wintering habitat for waterfowl and some shorebirds. The fragmented patchwork of pasture, woodlots, and suburban sprawl that now dominates most of this region creates significant bird conservation challenges.

30. New England/Mid-Atlantic Coast

This area has the densest human population of any region in the country. Much of what was formerly cleared for agriculture is now either in forest or in residential use. The highest priority birds are in coastal wetland and beach habitats, including the Saltmarsh Sharp-tailed Sparrow and Nelson's Sharp-tailed Sparrow, Seaside Sparrow, Piping Plover, American Oystercatcher, American Black Duck, and Black Rail. The region includes critical migration sites for Red Knot, Ruddy Turnstone, Sanderling, Semipalmated Sandpiper, and Dunlin. Most of the continental population of the endangered Roseate Tern nests on islands off the southern New England states. Other terns and gulls nest in large numbers, and large mixed colonies of herons, egrets, and ibis may form on islands in the Delaware and Chesapeake Bay regions. Estuarine complexes and embayments created behind barrier beaches in this region are extremely important to wintering and migrating waterfowl, including approximately 65 percent of the total wintering American Black Duck population, along with large numbers of Greater Scaup, Tundra Swan, Gadwall, Brant, and Canvasback. Exploitation and pollution of Chesapeake Bay and other coastal zones, and the accompanying loss of submerged aquatic vegetation, have significantly reduced their value to waterfowl.

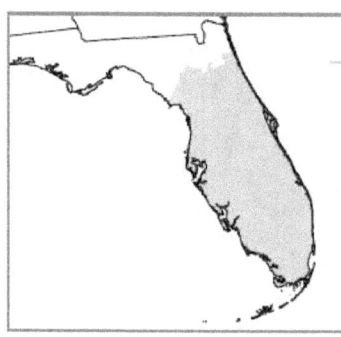

31. Peninsular Florida

The northern portion of Peninsular Florida is a transitional zone where the pine and bottomland hardwood elements of the Coastal Plain begin to merge with the tropical elements of south Florida. Many of the important pine and bottomland birds of the Coastal Plain, including Red-cockaded Woodpecker and Swallow-tailed Kite, extend into this area. The central scrub-oak Lake Wales Ridge is a center of endemism that includes all of the world's Florida Scrub-Jays. Colonies of Wood Stork, Glossy Ibis, and other herons and egrets are found throughout the region, while coastal islands support important continental breeding populations of Brown Pelicans, Black Skimmers, and various terns. Farther south, in the subtropical zone of the state, a normally frost-free climate creates conditions for mangroves, everglades, and tropical hammocks, tying this area more closely to the Bahamas and Caribbean than to the rest of the United States. Snail Kite, Short-tailed Hawk, and Limpkin breed in interior wetlands, with Mangrove Cuckoo and Black-whiskered Vireo in coastal mangroves. One of the greatest wading-bird concentrations in the world is in the Everglades. White-crowned Pigeons inhabit the Florida Keys, and the only Brown Noddy, Sooty Tern, and Magnificent Frigatebird breeding site in the country is on the Dry Tortugas. Wintering waterfowl abound in coastal waters, including large numbers of Lesser Scaup, Ring-necked Duck, and Green-winged Teal. The endemic Florida subspecies of Mottled Duck, Wood Duck, and Fulvous Whistling-Duck also breed in the area. Most of the remaining nesting Snowy Plovers in the Southeast occur along Florida's Gulf Coast. Extraordinary numbers of wintering and in-transit shorebirds also use the region, particularly Short-billed Dowitchers, but also Piping Plover, Dunlin, and Red Knot.

32. Coastal California

A Mediterranean climate of hot, dry summers and cool, moist winters creates conditions for mixed chaparral vegetation in the low mountains along the coast that extends into Baja California. These habitats support such birds as California Gnatcatcher, California Quail, Mountain Quail, Pygmy Nuthatch, Wrentit, California Thrasher, Nuttall's Woodpecker, Oak Titmouse, and Lawrence's Goldfinch. The coastline provides habitat for several waterfowl and shorebird species and is an important wintering area for Marbled Godwit, American Avocet, and Surfbird. Most of the world's populations of Ashy Storm-Petrel and Xantus' Murrelet nest on a small number of offshore islands. A sizable proportion of the Elegant Tern and Heermann's Gull populations spend the non-breeding season here. Millions of Sooty Shearwaters gather in pelagic waters each fall, joined by numbers of other shearwaters, storm-petrels, and alcids. The Central Valley of California lies in this region between the coastal ranges and the Sierra Nevada. Wetlands and associated uplands in the Central Valley provide roosting and foraging habitat for 60 percent of the waterfowl that winter in the Pacific Flyway, including a majority of the continental Northern Pintail population. Approximately 95 percent of the Central Valley's depressional wetlands and 84 percent of riparian habitat have been lost, primarily to agriculture. A good deal of the remaining wetland habitat is protected within national wildlife refuges, but the majority is privately managed for waterfowl hunting. Among landbirds, the Central Valley is the center of the small ranges of the Tricolored Blackbird and Yellow-billed Magpie and also provides dwindling habitat for a host of riparian birds, such as Least Bell's Vireo.

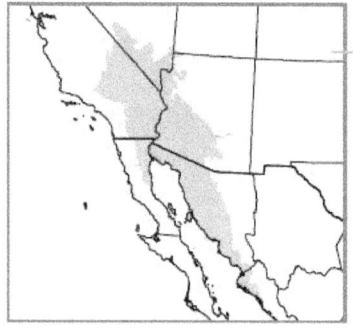

33. Sonoran and Mohave Deserts

The Mohave Desert covers southeastern California and southern Nevada and adjoins the Sonoran Desert, which extends from southwestern Arizona south on both sides of the Gulf of California into the Mexican states of Baja California, Sonora, and Sinaloa. This arid region is dominated by cacti, slow-growing grasses, creosote, and other desert shrubs. The Colorado River and adjacent wetlands provide habitat for ducks and other wetland birds, including some of the most important habitat in the arid southwest for Western and Clark's Grebes and American Avocets. This region also includes El Pinacate y Gran Desierto de Altar Biosphere Reserve in northern Mexico, which is a unique biome providing habitat for many raptors, such as Golden Eagle and wintering Northern Harrier, Short-eared Owl, and Merlin. Isla Tiburón, located off the coast of Sonora in the Gulf of California, is an IBA that harbors endemic forms of the Northern Flicker, Cactus Wren, and Xantus' Hummingbird and such pelagic birds as the Magnificent Frigatebird, Red-billed Tropicbird, Brown Booby, Blue-footed Booby, and Craveri's Murrelet. Another Mexican IBA, the Sistema Tóbari, supports large numbers of American Avocet, Marbled Godwit, Northern Pintail, and Lesser Scaup. This BCR is the center of distribution of the Rufous-winged Sparrow, LeConte's Trasher, Lucy's Warbler, and Abert's Towhee. Riparian wetlands are habitat for the Yuma Clapper Rail and Southwestern Willow Flycatcher. The Salton Sea hosts large numbers of American White Pelicans, Eared Grebes, and other colonial waterbirds; shorebirds, such as the Black-necked Stilt and Long-billed Curlew; and waterfowl during both migration and winter.

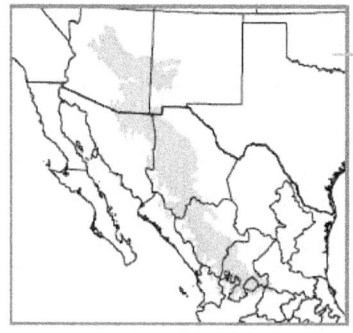

34. Sierra Madre Occidental

The Sierra Madre Occidental mountain range runs northwest to southeast parallel to the Pacific Coast from the Mogollon Rim and isolated mountain ranges in southeastern Arizona and southwestern New Mexico through Sonora to central Mexico, where it connects with the Sur del Altiplano Mexicano. It is characterized by high elevations and a complex topography with the presence of oak-pine, pine, and fir forests along the mountain range and of semiarid scrub habitats on eastern slopes. In Mexico there are more than 20 IBAs in this BCR, including El Carricito, a remnant of old-growth pine-oak forest and habitat for the presumably extinct Imperial Woodpecker and other important species, such as Golden Eagle, Military Macaw, Thick-billed Parrot, and Eared Trogon. Other priority landbirds of this BCR in Mexico are the Rose-throated Becard, Spotted Owl, Golden Eagle, and Peregrine Falcon. Among the species whose range extends into the United States in this region, highest priorities include the Red-faced Warbler, Strickland's Woodpecker, and Montezuma Quail. Riparian areas in lowlands support many in-transit migrants as well as breeding Thick-billed Kingbirds, Western Yellow-billed Cuckoos, and Southwestern Willow Flycatcher. Most uplands in the United States are publicly owned, but lower-elevation grasslands and riparian habitat are subject to development and conversion. The whole region is an important corridor for migration of many species in the west. Significant wetland habitats, such as Santi-aguillo Lagoon in Durango, Mexico, provide wintering habitat for large numbers of aquatic birds, highlighted by Northern Pintails and American White Pelicans.

35. Chihuahuan Desert

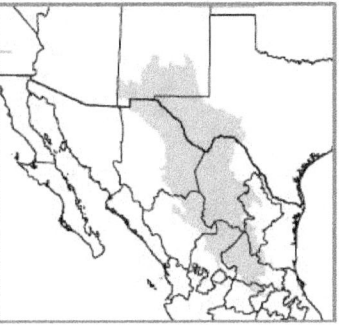

The Chihuahuan Desert stretches from the Sierra Madre Occidental in the west to lusher scrub habitat of the Edwards Plateau and Tamaulipan Brushlands in the east, and from the Southern Great Plains to the north and over much of the central Mexican Plateau. Arid grasslands and shrublands cover broad basins, and higher-elevation oak-juniper woodlands and conifers occur in numerous isolated mesas and mountains. In Mexico, IBAs include Janos–Nuevo Casas Grandes, home of the Burrowing Owl, Golden and Bald Eagles, Peregine and Prairie Falcons, Lucy's Warbler, and Mountain Plover. Sierra del Nido, with Eared Trogon, Thick-billed Parrot, and Lucifer's Hummingbird, and Mapimí are two other key IBAs. Other important typical species are Scaled Quail in the lowlands, Bell's Vireo along some riparian zones, and Black-capped Vireo in the montane scrub community. The Colima Warbler is a rare inhabitant of a few of the higher mountains. The Río Grande and adjacent wetlands provide important habitat for Sandhill Cranes, waterfowl, and other riparian and wetland-dependent birds.

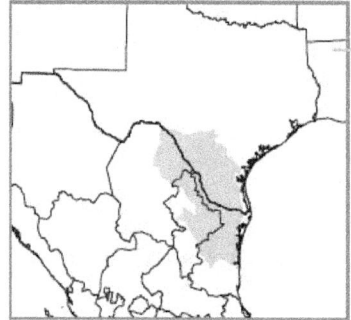

36. Tamaulipan Brushlands

This plain extends from southern Texas into northeastern Mexico. Much of the grassland, savanna, and thornscrub habitat has been converted to more shrubby conditions as a result of grazing history. Important Bird Areas in Mexico include Presa Venustiano Carranza, with nesting habitat for Mexican Ducks and Golden Eagles. It is also a key site for migrating Greater White-fronted Geese, Sandhill Cranes, and many species of ducks. Parras de la Fuente is an IBA that supports an important nesting colony of White-winged Dove and provides habitat for Red-crowned Parrot and Yellow-headed Parrot. Other distinctive avifauna of this region includes Audubon's Oriole, Buff-bellied Hummingbird, Long-billed Thrasher, and Plain Chachalaca. Botteri's Sparrow, Attwater's Prairie-Chicken, White-tailed Hawk, wintering Whooping Crane, and LeConte's Sparrow are high priority species of grassland habitats. Wetlands are habitat for Black-bellied Whistling-Ducks and a great variety of wading and shorebirds, as well as for several wintering waterfowl species.

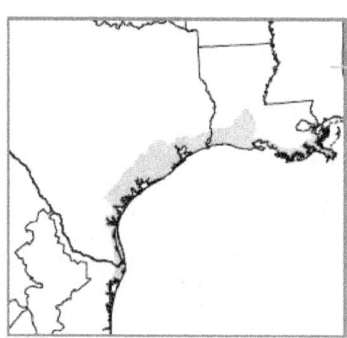

37. Gulf Coastal Prairie

Flat grasslands and marshes hug the coast of the Gulf of Mexico from northern Tamaulipas across the mouth of the Río Grande up into the rice country of southeastern Texas and southwestern Louisiana and across the great Louisiana marshlands at the mouth of the Mississippi River. The Laguna Madre on both sides of the border (an IBA in Mexico) is dominated by dunes, beaches, and black mangroves. This BCR features one of the greatest concentrations of colonial waterbirds in the world, with breeding Reddish Egret, Roseate Spoonbill, Brown Pelican, and large numbers of herons, egrets, ibis, terns, and skimmers. The region provides critical in-transit habitat for migrating shorebirds, including Buff-breasted Sandpiper and Hudsonian Godwit, and for most of the neotropical migrant forest birds of eastern North America. Mottled Duck, Fulvous Whistling-Duck, and Purple Gallinule also breed in wetlands, and winter numbers of waterfowl are among the highest on the continent. These include dabbling ducks (especially Northern Pintail and Gadwall), Redhead, Lesser Scaup, and White-fronted Geese from both the Central and the Mississippi Flyways. The most important waterfowl habitats of the area are coastal marsh, shallow estuarine bays and lagoons, and wetlands on agricultural lands of the rice prairies. Loss and degradation of wetland habitats due to subsidence, sea-level rise, shoreline erosion, freshwater and sediment deprivation, saltwater intrusion, oil and gas canals, and navigation channels and associated maintenance dredging are the most important problems facing the area's wetland wildlife.

38. Islas Marías

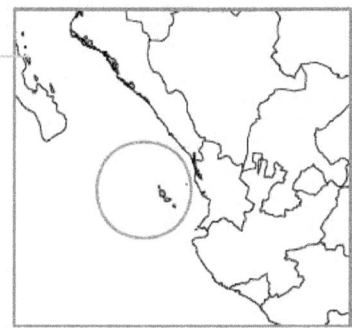

Located in the Pacific Ocean offshore from Nayarit, the Islas Marías (María Madre, María Magdalena, and María Cleofas) plus the near-shore Isla Isabel comprise this BCR. These islands range in elevation from sea level to 200 meters and are covered by tropical deciduous and subdeciduous forest. They are a center of endemism for birds at the subspecies level and provide habitat for the Red-breasted Chat, Mexican Parrotlet, Greenish Elaenia, Dusky-capped Flycatcher, Yellow-headed Parrot, Cinnamon Hummingbird, Broad-billed Hummingbird, Elegant Trogon, Pauraque, Happy Wren, Golden Vireo, Rose-throated Becard, Ladder-backed Woodpecker, Yellow-green Vireo, Tropical Parula, Flame-colored Tanager, and Hooded Oriole. Seabirds using the islands include the Magnificent Frigatebird, Red-billed Tropicbird, Brown Booby, Blue-footed Booby, and Sooty Tern.

39. Sierras de Baja California

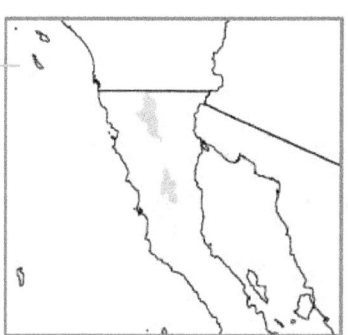

This BCR is comprised of the Sierra de Juárez and the Sierra de San Pedro Mártir, two similar IBAs located in northern Baja California. Vegetation types rise with elevation from Mediterranean chaparral to pine-oak and pine forests. High priority birds include Oak Titmouse, Wrentit, California Thrasher, Western Scrub-Jay, Rufous-crowned Sparrow, Bewick's Wren, California Towhee, Loggerhead Shrike, California Gnatcatcher, California Quail, Mountain Quail and Mountain Chickadee.

40. Desierto de Baja California

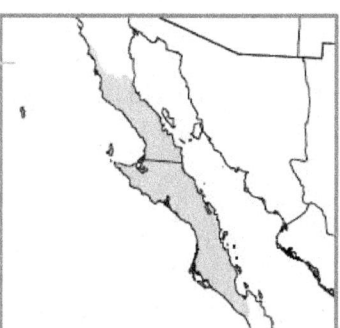

This BCR includes most of Baja California. It is a center of endemism that includes flat desert zones similar to the Sonoran Desert, shrublands, and coastal lagoons. The El Vizcaíno Biosphere Reserve—the largest reserve in Mexico and Latin America—is found here, as are several IBAs. The desert shrublands and salt marshes of Área de San Quintín provide habitat for California Gnatcatcher, Clapper Rail, Least Tern, Brant, and Western Sandpiper. Complejo Lagunar Ojo de Liebre and Complejo Lagunar San Ignacio IBAs are dominated by halophytic scrubs, salt marshes, and mangroves. These lagoon complexes are critical for shorebird and waterfowl species, such as Brant, Caspian and Royal Terns, Black-vented Shearwater, and Snowy Plover. Bahía Magdalena–Almejas IBA includes desert scrub and mangrove habitat for such birds as Elegant Tern, Bald Eagle, Northern Pintail, Blue-winged Teal, Lesser Scaup, Brown Pelican, Brandt's Cormorant, and a breeding colony of Magnificent Frigatebird. Sierra la Giganta IBA is dominated by desert scrub that is home to the endemic Xantus' Hummingbird and Gray Thrasher.

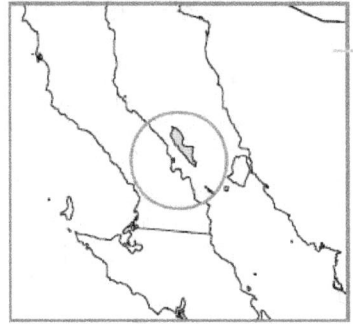

41. Islas del Golfo de California

This region includes about 100 islands and as many islets between the Colorado River delta and the 23rd parallel. The islands are important as a rich center of endemism. They provide nesting sites for many oceanic species and a corridor for migrants. The habitats are dominated by a dry desert climate with flora similar to that of the Sonoran Desert. Desert scrubland, mangrove, coastal dunes, and tropical deciduous forests are the most common habitat types. Isla Ángel de la Guarda, one of the largest islands in the Gulf of California, is an IBA that provides nesting habitat for Heermann's and Western Gulls, Brown Pelican, and Osprey. Archipiélago Loreto, an IBA that includes Isla Monserrat, Isla Catalina, and Isla Carmen, contains desert thorn-scrub, tropical deciduous forest, and dune habitats and columnar cacti that support Short-eared Owl, Red-tailed Hawk, Great-horned Owl, Peregrine Falcon, Hooded Oriole, Xantus' Hummingbird, Red-billed Tropicbird, and two endemic subspecies of Black-throated Sparrow.

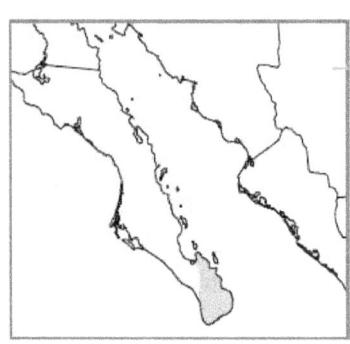

42. Sierra y Planicies de El Cabo

The southern tip of the Baja California peninsula includes the Sierra la Laguna, an area of desert scrubland and tropical deciduous forest. Endemic birds include Xantus' Hummingbird, Gray Thrasher, the San Lucas subspecies of American Robin, and Baird's Junco. Estero de San José IBA features palm groves, desert scrubland, salt marsh, mesquite, and aquatic vegetation. It is the last stopover for many aquatic birds and shorebirds during their migration to and from southern Mexico. Additional endemics are the Cape Pygmy-Owl and Belding's Yellowthroat.

43. Planicie Costera, Lomeríos y Cañones de Occidente

This BCR extends from eastern Sonora south to coastal Nayarit along the Pacific slope of the Sierra Madre Occidental. Vegetation is mainly thorn scrubland, tropical deciduous forest, and pine and oak forests, crossed by ribbons of riparian vegetation. Mangroves and other wetlands are found near the coast. Cuenca del Río Yaqui is a watershed IBA in southeastern Sonora having a unique combination of tropical and subtropical ravines (barrancas) that supports approximately 275 bird species, including Bare-throated Tiger-Heron, Black-bellied Whistling-Duck, Military Macaw, White-fronted Parrot, Whiskered Screech-Owl, Northern Pygmy-Owl,

Blue-throated and Costa's Hummingbirds, Strickland's Woodpecker, Thick-billed Kingbird, Rose-throated Becard, Black-
capped Gnatcatcher, Yellow-green Vireo, and Tropical Parula.
Alamos–Río Mayo is an IBA in southeastern Sonora and adjacent
Chihuahua that is the northern limit of tropical deciduous forests,
with such key species as the Lilac-crowned Parrot. San Juan de
Camarones is a western Durango IBA that includes the old-growth
pine forest of the highlands and descends along the typical Sierra
Madre Occidental Pacific slope gradient of pine, pine-oak, tropical
deciduous, and semi-deciduous forests and desert shrublands.
Important species in this IBA include the Golden Eagle, Thick-
billed Parrot, and Eared Trogon. Southward in coastal Sinaloa lies
the Ensenada Pabellones IBA, a large coastal lagoon covered by
mangroves and tule that provides winter habitat for the Greater
White-fronted Goose and important breeding habitat for Brown
Pelican, Osprey, and Magnificent Frigatebird. Bahía Santa María in
central Sinaloa is the most important wintering site for Brant on
the continental coast of Mexico. Also wintering here are American
White and Brown Pelicans, Green-winged Teal, Northern Pintail,
Northern Shoveler, Redhead, Lesser Scaup, Bufflehead, Greater
White-fronted Goose, Red-breasted Merganser, and Piping Plover.

44. Marismas Nacionales

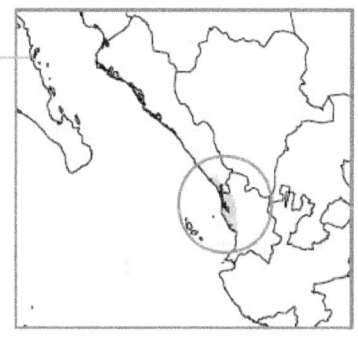

Marismas Nacionales, a Ramsar site located on the southern coast
of Sinaloa and adjacent Nayarit, is a complex mosaic of salty
coastal lagoons, mangroves, marshes, and swamps nurtured by
seven rivers. Vegetation includes mangroves, marshes, tropical
deciduous and semi-deciduous forests, and halophytic brushlands. More than 70,000 waterfowl and 100,000 shorebirds,
including migrants and residents, use this BCR. Key species are
Wood Stork, Black-bellied Whistling-Duck, Osprey, Mexican Parrotlet, Lilac-crowned Parrot, and Yellow-headed Parrot.

45. Planicie Costera y Lomeríos del Pacífico Sur

This BCR runs along the Pacific coast of Mexico from Nayarit
south through Chiapas. Vegetation typically includes tropical
deciduous and semi-deciduous forests, mangroves, desert scrublands, and riparian vegetation. Species endemic to this part of
Mexico include Lilac-crowned Parrot, Bumblebee Hummingbird,
Blue Mockingbird, West Mexican Chachalaca, Green-fronted
Hummingbird, Golden-crowned Emerald, Golden-cheeked Woodpecker, White-striped Woodcreeper, Flammulated Flycatcher, San
Blas Jay, Rufous-backed Robin, Golden Vireo, and Sinaloa and

Happy Wrens. The Chamela–Cuitzmala IBA is also a biosphere reserve and the locale for two biological stations. Additional important species found in the IBA include Black-vented Shearwater, Least Storm-Petrel, Elegant Tern, Peregrine Falcon, Yellow-headed Parrot, Military Macaw, Banded Quail, Mexican Parrotlet, Balsas Screech-Owl, Violet-crowned Hummingbird, Golden-cheeked Woodpecker, Black-capped Gnatcatcher, Blue Mockingbird, Red-headed Tanager, Orange-breasted Bunting, Black-chested Sparrow, Audubon's Oriole, and Yellow-winged Cacique. The coastal portion of the Coacolmán–Pómaro IBA is covered by tropical deciduous and semi-deciduous forests. Species associated with the well-preserved altitudinal gradient include Reddish Egret, Wood Stork, Common Black-Hawk, Sharp-shinned Hawk, Great Black-Hawk, Peregrine Falcon, and Mottled Owl. Two small islands (Isla Redonda and Isla Larga), which lie just a few kilometers off the Nayarit–Jalisco coast, form the Islas Marietas IBA. Cliffs, caves, and sandy beaches ring the islands, with interior vegetation dominated by grasslands and columnar cacti. Large numbers of breeding birds congregate here, including more than half of Mexico's Bridled Tern, as well as Brown Boobies and Brown Noddies. Laguna de Manialtepec is a coastal Oaxaca IBA covered with aquatic and subaquatic vegetation, tropical deciduous forest, thorn forest, mangroves, coastal dunes, and palm plantations. Important species include Townsend's Shearwater, Red-footed Booby, Least Bittern, Reddish Egret, Wood Stork, Muscovy Duck, Northern Pintail, Blue-winged Teal, Masked Duck, Yellow-headed Vulture, Crane Hawk, Elegant and Least Terns, and Cinnamon-tailed Sparrow.

46. Sur del Altiplano Mexicano

The Altiplano Sur is located in central Mexico, occupying parts of the states of Querétaro, Hidalgo, Guanajuato, and Michoacán. This region's historic landscape has been transformed by human settlements, agriculture, forestry, and cattle ranching. It is now characterized by shrublands and mixed forests. The BCR's only IBA, Sierra de Santa Rosa, has 14 different oak species and provides habitat for priority birds, such as Ocellated Thrasher, Violet-crowned Hummingbird, Rufous-backed Robin, Russet Nightingale-Thrush, Red Warbler, Blue Mockingbird, Aztec Thrush, and Worthen's Sparrow.

47. Eje Neovolcánico Transversal

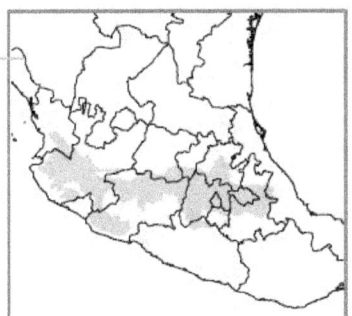

The Tranverse Volcanic Belt runs west to east through the states of Jalisco, Nayarit, Colima, Guerrero, Michoacán, Guanajuato, Querétaro, Morelos, Hidalgo, Distrito Federal, México, Tlaxcala, Puebla, and Veracruz. This is an extensive volcanic mountain range that includes the highest elevations in Mexico, including the Pico de Orizaba in Veracruz (5,747 meters), Popocatépetl (5,452 meters) and Iztccíhuatl (5,146 meters) on the border between Puebla and México, and Nevado de Colima (4,625 meters) on the Colima–Jalisco border. This region separates the Central Plateau from the Balsas Basin and is characterized by pine, pine-oak, and fir forests and temperate grasslands. Valleys and basins amid this complex are sites for some of the country's largest cities, including la Ciudad de México, Guadalajara, Toluca, and Morelia. La Malinche is an isolated mountain and one of the oldest volcanoes in the Eje Neovolcánico. Vegetation is primarily pine and pine-fir forests and grasslands. Endemic species include Rufous-capped Brush-Finch, Red Warbler, Russet Nightingale-Thrush, and Striped Sparrow. Volcanes Iztaccíhuatl and Popocatépetl are located near la Ciudad de México within the states of México, Puebla, and Morelos. Additional endemic species here include the White-napped Swift, Long-tailed Wood-Partridge, Bumblebee Hummingbird, Gray-barred Wren, Spotted Wren, Rufous-backed Robin, Ocellated Thrasher, Blue Mocking-bird, Hooded Yellowthroat, Green-striped Brush-Finch, and Rusty-crowned Ground-Sparrow. Sierra de Taxco–Nevado de Toluca IBA, located in México and adjacent Guerrero, includes a large area of well-preserved cloud forest. Important birds here include Solitary Eagle, Slaty Vireo, Spotted and Gray-barred Wrens, and White-striped Woodcreeper. Sur del Valle de México is an IBA in Distrito Federal and Morelos. Additional priority birds in this IBA include the Stygian Owl, Ferruginous Pygmy-Owl, Black-vented Oriole, Sierra Madre Sparrow, and Aztec Thrush. Lago de Cuitzeo IBA in Michoacán is covered by halophytic grass-lands, aquatic and subaquatic vegetation, and tropical deciduous forests. This IBA contains one of the most important wetlands in central Mexico. Endemic Black-polled Yellowthroats and threat-ened Dwarf Vireos and Least Bitterns are found here.

48. Sierra Madre Oriental

The Sierra Madre Oriental is a north-south mountain range in eastern Mexico that passes through parts of the states of Coahuila, Nuevo León, Tamaulipas, San Luis Potosí, Querétaro, Hidalgo, Veracruz, and Puebla. It divides the Central Plateau from the Eastern Coastal Plains and is dominated by oak, pine-oak, and pine forests, cloud forests, tropical semi-deciduous forests, and dry scrublands. El Cielo IBA, located on the Gulf slope of the Sierra Madre, is covered by diverse vegetation types that host 400 bird species (56 percent residents, 46 percent winter visitors). Included among these species are 13 endemic species and populations of globally important Military Macaw, Maroon-fronted Parrot, and Red-crowned Parrot. San Antonio Peña Nevada IBA in southwestern Nuevo León includes desert scrubland and pine and oak forest habitats used by the Maroon-fronted Parrot. San Nicolás de los Montes in San Luis Potosí consists of tropical semi-deciduous and oak forests and is habitat for the endemic Russet Nightingale-Thrush, Hooded Yellowthroat, and Crimson-collared Grosbeak, as well as Bat Falcon, Hooded and Audubon's Orioles, and Blue Mockingbird. Sierra Gorda IBA in Querétaro and adjacent San Luis Potosí consists of a remarkable variety of vegetation types, including tropical deciduous and semi-deciduous forests, desert scrubland, cloud forest, and oak, pine-oak, and pine forests. Important species include Military Macaw, Great Curassow, Crested Guan, Bearded Wood-Partridge, White-crowned Parrot and Emerald Toucanet, Red-crowned Parrot, Bumblebee Hummingbird, Tamaulipan Crow, Spotted Wren, and Rufous-capped Brushfinch.

49. Planicie Costera y Lomeríos Secos del Golfo de México

This BCR lies along the Gulf of Mexico in southern Tamaulipas, adjacent Veracruz, and northeastern San Luis Potosí, with a second portion in central Veracruz. Vegetation includes tropical deciduous and semi-deciduous forests, thorn forests, aquatic and subaquatic vegetation, grasslands, desert scrubland, and portions of cloud forest and oak forest. Sierra de Tamaulipas is an isolated zone on the coastal plain rising to 1,500 meters. Because of its isolation, it is an area of high endemism for plants and a refuge for many vertebrates, including the Great Black Hawk, Roadside Hawk, Yellow-headed Parrot, Red-lored Parrot, Red-crowned Parrot, Green Parakeet, Eastern Screech-Owl, Crimson-collared Grosbeak, Chihuahuan Raven, Golden-crowned Warbler, and wintering Black-throated Green Warbler. Sierra del Abra Tanchipa in San Luis Potosí is the northern limit of tropical deciduous and

palm forests. Birds here include Military Macaw, Tamaulipan
Crow, Wild Turkey, Plain Chachalaca, Lazuli Bunting, and Eastern
Towhee. Presa Vicente Guerrero is a reservoir surrounded by well-
preserved Tamaulipan scrubland and tropical deciduous forest.
Species registered here include Crested Guan, Black-bellied
Whistling-Duck, Muscovy Duck, numerous wintering temperate
duck species, and White-tipped Dove.

50. Cuenca del Río Balsas

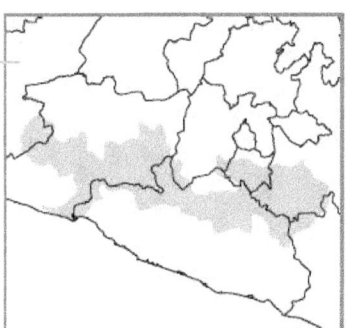

The Balsas River Basin is located in Morelos, Oaxaca, Guerrero,
Puebla, and Michoacán. It is limited to the north and east by the
Eje Neovolcánico, to the south by the Sierra Madre del Sur, and
to the east by the Valle de Tehuacán–Cuicatlán and Sierra Norte
de Puebla–Oaxaca. Vegetation includes tropical deciduous forests
and desert scrubland. Sierra de Huautla in Morelos provides habitat for Common Black Hawk, Ferruginous Pygmy-Owl, Pileated
Flycatcher, Black-vented Oriole, Hooded Oriole, Blue Mockingbird,
Rusty-crowned Ground-Sparrow, Happy Wren, West Mexican
Chachalaca, Golden-cheeked and Gray-breasted Woodpeckers,
Dusky Hummingbird, and Blue Seedeater. Cuenca Baja del Balsas,
an IBA in southeast Michoacán and adjacent Guerrero, is a depres-
sion covered by tropical vegetation. It includes the Infiernillo
Reservoir, which is important for waterfowl. Additional priority
birds here include Wood Stork, Great Black Hawk, Banded Quail,
Military Macaw, Flammulated Flycatcher, Rufous-backed Robin,
and wintering Black-capped Vireo. Cañón del Zopilote is an IBA
in central Guerrero typified by tropical deciduous forest, desert
scrubland, and columnar cacti. Belted Flycatcher, Balsas Screech-
Owl, and Black-chested Sparrow are found in the habitats of this
IBA.

51. Valle de Tehuacán–Cuicatlán

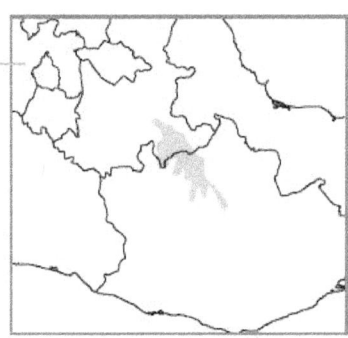

Located in the states of Puebla and Oaxaca, Valle de Tehuacán–
Cuicatlán is covered by a desert scrubland that hosts almost 3,000
species of vascular plants. This BCR is considered a center of
endemism and diversification of columnar cacti (45 of 70 known
species in the world). Almost 30 percent of flora is endemic. This
region is a biosphere reserve that contains a mixture of species
from arid regions of North America and from tropical humid
montane regions. Priority species include Boucard's Wren; West
Mexican Chachalaca; Lucifer, Beautiful, and Dusky Hummingbirds; Gray-breasted Woodpecker; Ocellated Thrasher; Slaty and
Dwarf Vireos; White-throated Towhee; and Bridled and Oaxaca
Sparrows.

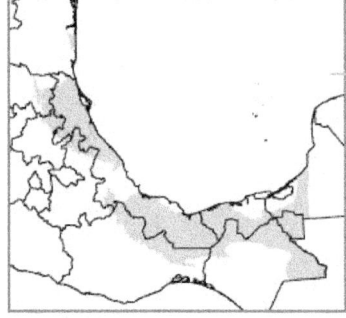

52. Planicie Costera y Lomeríos Húmedos del Golfo de México

This BCR has the shape of a half moon, beginning in central Veracruz and extending southeast through Tabasco, north through Oaxaca and Chiapas, and east through Campeche. Vegetation includes tropical evergreen, semi-deciduous and deciduous forests, thorn forest, oak and pine forests, grasslands, and extensive areas of early successional growth and agriculture. Humedales del Sur de Tamaulipas y Norte de Veracruz is an IBA in southern Tamaulipas and adjacent Veracruz vegetated by thorn forest, introduced grasslands, agricultural lands, and flooded areas with halophytic vegetation. Wintering migrants make up 45 percent of the avifauna, including many species of waterfowl. There are also six Mexican endemic species here: Green Parakeet, Red-crowned Parrot, Bronze-winged Woodpecker, Tamaulipan Crow, Altamira Yellowthroat, and Crimson-collared Grosbeak. Humedales de Alvarado is a central Veracruz IBA that consists of a coastal system of dunes with desert scrubland patches, mangroves, and tropical deciduous and semi-deciduous forests. Again, many of the important birds here are wintering migrants associated with wetlands, including Piping Plover, Yellow-headed Vulture, Snail Kite, Least Bittern, Northern Pintail, American White Pelican, Common Black Hawk, and Black-collared Hawk. Uxpanapa, part of the Coatzacoalcos River Basin, is another IBA located on the border between Veracruz and Oaxaca. The original vegetation in the western portion has been transformed, but important extensions of tropical rainforests remain in the east. Important species include Long-tailed Sabrewing; Slender-billed Wren; Great, Little, Thicket, and Slaty-breasted Tinamous; Hook-billed, White-tailed, and Plumbeus Kites; Crane and White Hawks; Bat and Laughing Falcons; Plain Chachalaca; Pale-vented Pigeon; Blue Ground-Dove; Gray-fronted Dove; White-crowned and Mealy Parrots; Squirrel and Striped Cockoos; Green Shrike-Vireo; Rufous-browed Peppershrike; Tropical Parula; and a host of wintering warblers (Magnolia, Black-throated Green, Black-and-white, Worm-eating, and Kentucky Warblers, Ovenbird, and American Redstart). El Ocote IBA in the Grijalba Basin River of northwestern Chiapas is covered with tropical rainforest and tropical deciduous and semi-deciduous forests, thorn forest, pine and oak forests, grasslands, and agricultural lands. This center of biodiversity includes Nava's Wren, Emerald-chinned Hummingbird, Singing Quail, Chestnut-headed and Montezuma Oropendolas, and Plain Xenops.

53. Sierra Madre del Sur

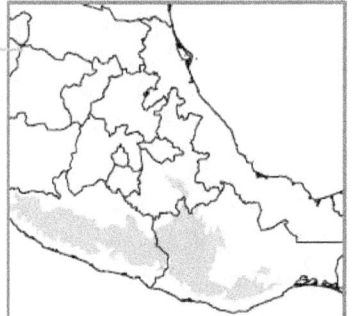

Sierra Madre del Sur borders the Pacific coast from the Eje Neovol-cánico to the Istmo de Tehuantepec, extending about 1,200 kilo-meters through the states of Jalisco, Colima, Michoacán, Guerrero, and Oaxaca. One of the many IBAs in this region, Sierra de Miahu-atlán, is a mountain range in southern Oaxaca dominated by tropi-cal semi-deciduous forest, cloud forest, and pine-oak forest. Birds that have been reported for this mountain range include White-throated Jay, Blue-capped Hummingbird, Black-capped Vireo, White-naped Swift, Long-tailed Wood-Partridge, Rufous-bellied Chachalaca, West-Mexican Chachalaca, Cinnamon Hummingbird, and the Blue-capped Hummingbird (the latter being endemic to Miahuatlán). The vegetation of Acahuizotla–Agua del Obispo in Guerrero consists of tropical deciduous and semi-deciduous forests, pine forest, and grasslands. Additional endemic birds here include Eared Poorwill, Gray-crowned Woodpecker, Barred Wood-creeper, Emerald Toucanet, Green-fronted Hummingbird, Flam-mulated Flycatcher, Rosy Thrush-Tanager, Red-headed Tanager, Collared Towhee, and Dwarf Vireo. Sierra de Atoyac IBA includes Cerro Teotepec, the highest peak in Guerrero at 3,705 meters. Vegetation is tropical semi-deciduous, cloud, and coniferous forests. Additional endemic species include Scaled Antpitta, Russet Nightingale-Thrush, Unicolored Jay, Sinaloa Wren, Happy Wren, and Golden Vireo. Threatened species include Ornate Hawk-Eagle, Black Hawk-Eagle, Bat Falcon, Singing Quail, Short-crested Coquette, White-throated Jay, White-tailed Hummingbird, and Yellow-headed Parrot. Omiltemi is another Guerrero IBA. This one consists of a series of humid canyons covered with pine-oak, cloud, tropical deciduous, and tropical semi-deciduous forests. This very isolated area is a center of endemism and species rich-ness, including several bird species of restricted distribution and/or many endangered species. Among these are the White-throated Jay, White-tailed Hummingbird, White-striped Woodcreeper, Long-tailed Wood-Partridge, Aztec Thrush, and Emerald Toucanet.

54. Sierra Norte de Puebla–Oaxaca

This BCR, crossing through northern Oaxaca and adjacent eastern Puebla and western Veracruz, is a major landmark due to its abrupt relief and numerous peaks rising to 3,000 meters. Vegeta-tion includes coniferous, cloud, and tropical deciduous forests. Sierra Norte is an IBA that rises in elevation to 3,700 meters in Cerro de Cempoaltepetl. Habitats include tropical rainforest; trop-ical deciduous, semi-deciduous, cloud, and oak and pine forests; desert brushlands; and grasslands. Priority birds are Dwarf Jay, Slender-billed Wren, Oaxaca Sparrow, Keel-billed Motmot, and

Yellow-headed Parrot. Unión–Chinanteca in north-central Oaxaca is part of a complex and abrupt mountain system having a vast mosaic of different vegetation types, including coniferous, cloud, and tropical semi-deciduous forests. Additional endemic bird species include Long-tailed Sabrewing, Long-tailed Wood-Partridge, Ocellated Thrasher, Red Warbler, Boucard's Wren, Rufous-capped Brush-Finch, and White-naped Brush-Finch. The Great Curassow, Chestnut-headed Oropendola, and White Hawk are among the threatened species present.

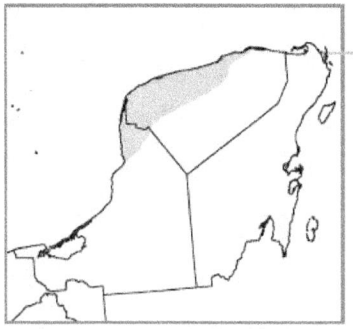

55. Planicie Noroccidental de Yucatán

This BCR lies along the coastal areas of northern Campeche and northwestern Yucatán. It is dominated by coastal dunes, mangrove swamps, halophytic grasslands, tropical deciduous forests, thorn forests, and bulrushes. Los Petenes is a large swamp system that includes mangroves and tropical deciduous and subdeciduous forests on flooded plains. Bird species reported include the Orange Oriole, Hooded Oriole, Yellow-lored Parrot, Jabiru, Wood Stork, Muscovy Duck, Ferruginous Pygmy-Owl, Least Bittern, Reddish Egret, Snail Kite, Bat Falcon, King Vulture, Black Hawk-Eagle, and such wintering waterfowl as Blue-winged Teal, Northern Pintail, American Wigeon, and Lesser Scaup. Ría Celestún is a biosphere reserve located on the northern coast of Campeche and western Yucatán. It is an area of saline wetlands and coastal lagoons. Habitats include mangroves (red, black, and white), marshes, coastal dunes, and tropical subdeciduous forests. Important species include Ocellated Turkey, Yucatan Poorwill, Yucatan Wren, Yucatan Jay, Least Tern, Greater Flamingo, Muscovy Duck, Yellow-headed Vulture, Common Black Hawk, White-tailed Hawk, Limpkin, and Piping Plover, along with wintering waterfowl. Ichka 'Ansijo IBA on the coast of Yucatán includes coastal dune, mangrove swamp, halophytic grassland, bulrush, tropical deciduous forest, and lowland thorn forest habitats. Additional birds of interest include Great Curassow, Burrowing Owl, Crane Hawk, and Peregrine Falcon.

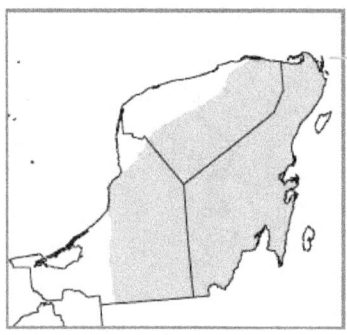

56. Planicie de la Península de Yucatán

This BCR covers most of the Yucatan Peninsula, including parts of Campeche and Quintana Roo and all of Yucatán. Calakmul is an IBA and biosphere reserve located at the highest elevations of the Campeche Plains. There are no major watercourses in the area, but rather surface pools, locally known as "aguadas," where water collects in natural depressions. Tropical semi-deciduous and deciduous forests, tropical rainforest, and aquatic vegetation predominate. This is the largest reserve in the Mexican tropics, sheltering an avifauna that includes 118 protected species and nine that are endemic to the region. Important among these are Harpy Eagle, King Vulture, Emerald Toucanet, Wood Stork, Jabiru, Muscovy Duck, Masked Duck, and Spectacled Owl. Mesoamerican endemics include Ocellated Turkey, Yellow-lored Parrot, Rose-throated Tanager, Red-vented Woodpecker, Orange Oriole, Yucatan Flycatcher, Yucatan Jay, and Yucatan Poorwill. Sierra de Ticul–Punto Put is an IBA at the point of convergence of the states of Campeche, Yucatán, and Quintana Roo. It is adjacent to Calakmul and has similar vegetation. Additional important species in this IBA include Common Black-Hawk, Great Curassow, Crested Guan, Yellow-headed Vulture, Bat Falcon, Limpkin, and wintering Hooded and Swainson's Warblers. Sian Ka'an IBA is also a biosphere reserve. It is located in coastal Quintana Roo and features a wide variety of habitat types, including tropical rainforest sloping down to the sea, flooded rainforests, freshwater and brackish swamps, coastal lagoons, and keys. Additional important species here include Rose-throated Tanager and Buff-bellied Hummingbird. This BCR also includes the Ría Lagartos Biosphere Reserve, where nesting Greater Flamingos are found.

57. Isla Cozumel

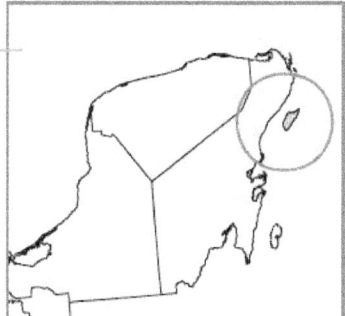

Isla Cozumel is located 17.5 kilometers off the northeastern coast of the Yucatan Peninsula. This large, flat island is affected by hurricanes at a frequency of one every 6.2 years. The habitats are those of tropical rainforest, tropical deciduous forest, mangrove swamp, bulrushes, and coastal dunes. Early successional vegetation is found in areas of human disturbance or in those areas recently affected by hurricanes. Most of the island area is uninhabited. Most agricultural and livestock activities are restricted to small areas, and a large part of the island is a reserve. The avifauna has a distinctive Caribbean influence, as evidenced by Stripe-headed Tanagers, White-crowned Pigeons, and wintering Palm and Black-throated Blue Warblers. Endemic birds include the Cozumel Thrasher, Cozumel Vireo, and Cozumel Wren; endemic subspecies include Great Curassow and Black Catbird. Other important species are Roseate Spoonbill, Osprey, Greater Flamingo, Reddish Egret, Blue-winged Teal, Masked Duck, Merlin, Peregrine Falcon, Least Tern, Yellow-lored Parrot, and wintering Hooded Warbler.

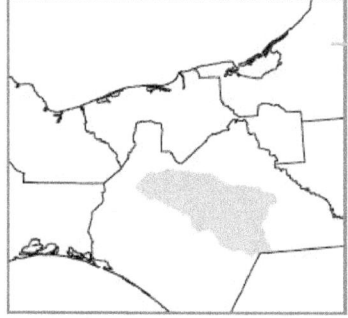

58. Altos de Chiapas

The highlands of central Chiapas run parallel to the Pacific Coast and extend to the lowlands of Selva Lacandona in a series of deep folds known as "cañadas." Cerro Saybal–Cerro Cavahlná is a mountainous IBA in the northern part of this BCR that is covered with cloud and pine-oak-liquidambar forests. Important birds noted here include Highland Guan, Singing Quail, Blue-throated Motmot, Azure-hooded Jay, and Wine-throated Hummingbird. Cerro Blanco, la Yerbabuena y Jotolchén is an IBA with vegetation similar to that in the area known as Selva Negra. Birds at this IBA include Resplendent Quetzal, Blue-throated Motmot, Black-throated Jay, Slaty Finch, and wintering Golden-cheeked Warbler. Cerros de San Cristóbal de las Casas IBA consists of pine-oak, oak, and cloud forests, and early successional vegetation. Additional birds here include Belted Flycatcher, Black-capped Siskin, White-throated Hummingbird, Slender Sheartail, and Emerald-chinned Hummingbird. Lagos de Montebello IBA in central Chiapas is dominated by pine-oak-liquidambar forest, with some patches of cloud forest in humid portions. Limpkin, White-crowned Parrot, Emerald Toucanet, and White-breasted Hawk are threatened or restricted-distribution birds found in this IBA.

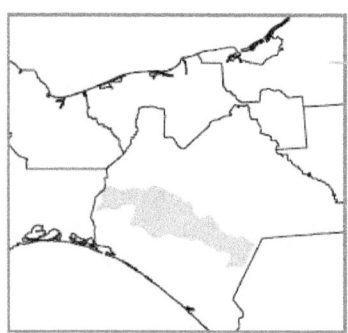

59. Depresiones Intermontanas

This BCR is a lowland corridor about 250 kilometers long and 75 kilometers wide that is bound on its two sides by the mountain ranges of Chiapas. Vegetation includes that of cloud forests, tropical rainforests, and tropical deciduous forests. The Zapotal–Mactumatza IBA includes priority species, such as Plain Chachalaca, Crested Guan, Great Curassow, Northern Bobwhite, Gray-necked Wood-Rail, Red-billed Pigeon, White-tipped Dove, Green Parakeet, Orange-fronted Parakeet, Mangrove Cuckoo, Squirrel Cuckoo, Lesser Ground-Cuckoo, Lesser Roadrunner, Tawny-collared Nightjar, Great Potoo, White-collared Swift, Vaux's Swift, Lesser Swallow-tailed Swift, White-throated Swift, Fork-tailed Emerald, Berylline Hummingbird, White-bellied Emerald, Plain-capped Starthroat, Violaceus Trogon, Collared Aracari, Yellow-bellied Sapsucker, Northern Bentbill, Yellow-olive Flycatcher, Belted Flycatcher, Sulphur-bellied Flycatcher, Gray-breasted Martín, Spotted-breasted Wren, Banded Wren, Plain Wren, Solitary Vireo, Lesser Greenlet, Fan-tailed Warbler, and wintering Western Tanager and Townsend's, Chestnut-sided, Magnolia, and Black-and-white Warblers. The IBA Corredor Laguna Bélgica-Sierra Limón-Cañón Sumidero consists of cloud forest, tropical rainforest, and tropical deciduous forest. A total of 215 bird species have been reported in this IBA. Threatened species include Highland Guan, Crested Owl, Emerald Toucanet, Keel-billed Toucan, Nava's Wren, and wintering Golden-cheeked Warbler.

60. Sierra Madre de Chiapas

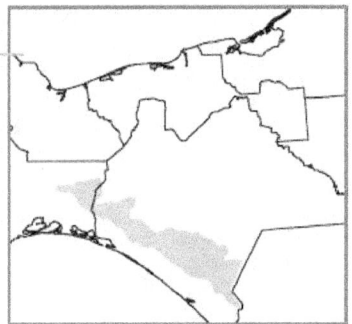

This BCR, on the Pacific coast of Chiapas, contains Mexico's oldest mountain range. A 4,026-meter volcano on the Mexico-Guatemala border defines the El Tacaná IBA. It is vegetated by cloud forest and scrubland. Important species include Bar-winged Oriole, Mountain Robin, Pink-headed Warbler, Resplendent Quetzal, Unspotted Saw-whet Owl, White-throated Swift, Lesser Swallow-tailed Swift, Greater Swallow-tailed Swift, Rufous Sabrewing, Violet Sabrewing, Green Violet-ear, Emerald-chinned Hummingbird, Mountain Trogon, Collared Trogon, Slaty-tailed Trogon, Blue-throated Motmot, Barred Antshrike, Eye-ringed Flatbill, Orange-billed Nightingale-Thrush, Ruddy-capped Nightingale-Thrush, Spotted Nightingale-Thrush, Crescent-chested Warbler, and wintering Wood Thrush and Townsend's and Hermit Warblers. La Sepultura IBA is considered a transitional zone between the Neartic and Neotropical Regions and a Pleistocenic haven. There are nine vegetation types with many endemic and rare plant species. Endemic bird species include Rose-bellied Bunting and Giant Wren. Threatened birds include Resplendent Quetzal, Rose-bellied Bunting, King Vulture, Solitary Eagle, White-crowned Parrot, and wintering Golden-cheeked Warbler. El Triunfo Biosphere Reserve is also designated an IBA, which is covered with cloud forest, tropical deciduous forest, coniferous forest, a relict oak forest on a small crest, grassland, and agricultural land. Three hundred ninety birds have been counted in this area, including Azure-rumped Tanager, Horned Guan, Resplendent Quetzal, Wine-throated Hummingbird, and Highland Guan.

61. Planicie Costera del Soconusco

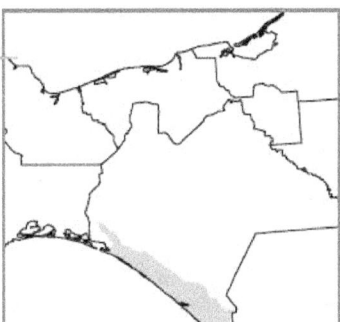

This BCR on the Pacific coast of Chiapas encompasses La Encrucijada, a biosphere reserve and an IBA. It has two large wetlands formed by rivers, lagoons, and estuaries. Vegetation includes tropical deciduous and subdeciduous forests, various wetland types, dunes, coastal scrublands, and the tallest mangroves in Mesoamerica. This is one of the most important systems of tropical wetlands on the Pacific Coast of North America and is the habitat of many rare, threatened, and endangered species. Birds of priority are the Magnificent Frigatebird; Wood Stork; Plain, West-Mexican, and White-bellied Chachalaca; 15 raptor species, including Snail Kite, Common Black-Hawk, Crane Hawk, Black-collared Hawk, Gray-headed Kite, and Peregrine Falcon; 13 duck species, including Muscovy Duck, Blue-winged Teal, and Redhead; 15 heron and egret species, including the Boat-billed Heron and Roseate Spoonbill; 20 shorebird and wading bird species, including Sungrebe, Limpkin, Snowy Plover, Black-bellied Plover, Wilson's Plover,

American Avocet, Northern Jacana, Greater Yellowlegs, Solitary Sandpiper, Whimbrel, Sanderling, and Western Sandpiper; and parakeets and parrots, including Green Parakeet, Orange-fronted Parakeet, Orange-chinned Parakeet, White-fronted Parrot, and Yellow-headed Parrot. Other important species include Giant Wren, Rufous-naped Wren, Mangrove Vireo, Bell's Vireo, Magnolia Warbler, American Redstart, Ovenbird, Northern Waterthrush, Yellow-breasted Chat, Indigo Bunting, and Painted Bunting.

62. Archipiélago de Revillagigedo

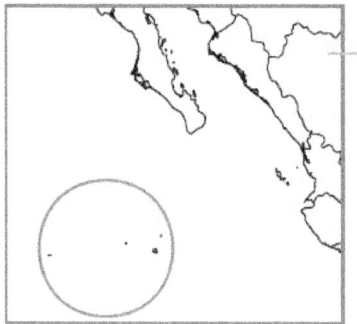

The Islas Revillagigedo off the Pacific coast of Colima is the most remote archipelago of Mexico. Four volcanic islands—Socorro, Clarión, San Benedicto, and Roca Partida—have a combined surface area of almost 40,000 hectares. Clarión and Socorro stand out for their wealth of endemic flora and fauna. Vegetation on Isla Socorro consists of *Croton* scrub, *Ficus cotinifolia* forest, and pine forest, with associated elements of cloud forest. Clarión is primarily scrub and scrub forest, while San Benedicto Island is covered by volcanic ash and plants that are recolonizing after a major eruption that took place in August 1952. Roca Partida Island is a rock island without vegetation. Endemic species include Townsend's Shearwater, Socorro Mockingbird, Socorro Parakeet, Socorro Dove, Clarion Wren, Socorro Wren, and Socorro Towhee.

63. Isla Guadalupe

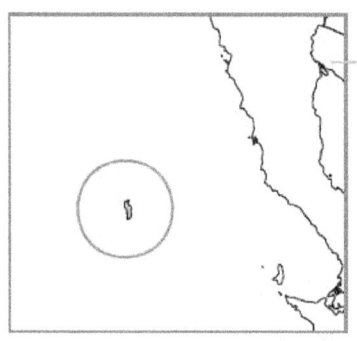

Isla Guadalupe is part of a volcanic archipelago located off the coast of Baja California. Its geomorphology is marked by steep slopes linked with a mountainous topography, with elevations up to 1,400 meters. Vegetation is xerophytic scrubland (matorral) and forests of an endemic cypress associated with pine and oak. Endemic birds include the Guadalupe Junco, Guadalupe Storm-Petrel, and subspecies of American Kestrel and Rock Wren. Other important species include Laysan Albatross (which breeds here), Red-billed Tropicbird, Heermann's Gull, Cassin's Auklet, and Burrowing Owl. Extinct forms are the endemic subspecies of Crested Caracara, Bewick's Wren, Spotted Towhee, and probably Guadalupe Storm-Petrel.

64. Arrecife Alacranes

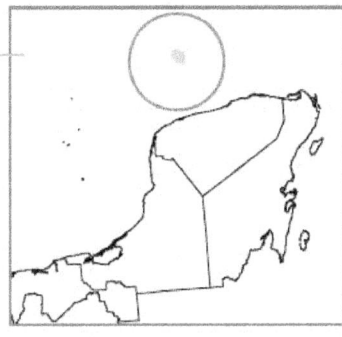

Arrecife Alacranes is located in the Gulf of Mexico northwest from the Yucatan Peninsula. It is a protected area of 88,084 hectares, including five islets (Isla Desertora, Isla Pájaros, Isla Desterrada, Isla Chica, and Isla Pérez) and the waters surrounding them. Vegetation consists basically of dunes and scrub habitat. This BCR is the most important breeding site in the Gulf of Mexico for Sooty Tern, and an important breeding area for Brown Noddy and Masked and Brown Boobies. Many birds migrating across the gulf stop here in fall and spring.

65. Los Tuxtlas

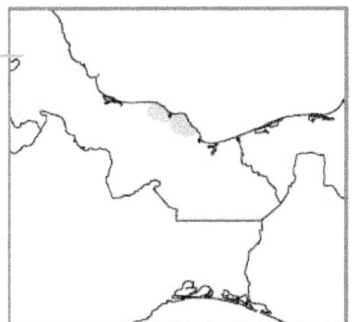

This region on the coast of central Veracruz is a biosphere reserve that includes Volcán de San Martín Tuxtla and the Sierra de Santa Martha. Vegetation is that of tropical rainforest, cloud and pine forests, early successional growth, grassland, coastal dune, and mangrove. Five hundred sixty-four bird species have been reported in Los Tuxtlas, including two species found only in this area: the Long-tailed Sabrewing and Tuxtla Quail-Dove. Other important resident species include Agami Heron, Crested Guan, Orange-breasted Falcon, Black Robin, White-throated Robin, Mangrove Vireo, and Rufous-browed Peppershrike. High priority wintering birds include Wood Thrush, Yellow-throated Vireo, Northern Parula, Magnolia Warbler, Black-throated Green Warbler, Yellow-throated Warbler, Worm-eating Warbler, Ovenbird, Northern Waterthrush, Louisiana Waterthrush, Kentucky Warbler, and Hooded Warbler.

66. Pantanos de Centla–Laguna de Términos

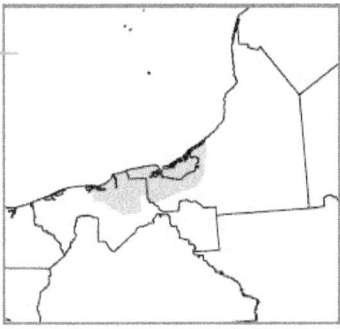

This BCR includes two IBAs and encompasses part of a biosphere reserve and a Ramsar site (Pantanos de Centla). Located in the Delta of Usumacinta–Grijalva Rivers, the area is a complex hydrological system of rivers, lagoons, swamps, and salt marshes. Habitats are tropical rainforest, bloodwood tree woodland, mangrove swamp, rosewood scrub, and palmetto grove. Some of the important birds here include Jabiru, Wood Stork, Yellow-headed Vulture, Common Black-Hawk, Great Black-Hawk, Muscovy Duck, Northern Pintail, Blue-winged Teal, Roadside Hawk, Bat Falcon, Limpkin, White-crowned Parrot, Ferruginous Pygmy-Owl, Hooded Warbler, Hooded Oriole, Orange Oriole, and Snail Kite.

67. Hawaii

This chain of volcanic islands is the richest area for endemic land-birds in the United States. Because of significant disturbances from introduced species, including disease-bearing mosquitoes, and conversion of large areas to agriculture or other uses, Hawaii also has the nation's highest concentration of endangered species. About 12 forest birds in the chain became extinct during the 20th century, and many others are very close to that brink. The main island chain supports important seabird breeding populations, including the endangered Dark-rumped Petrel and Newell's Shearwater. The Leeward Islands host immense numbers of nesting seabirds, including important colonies of Black-footed and Laysan Albatrosses; Bonin Petrels; boobies; frigatebirds; and Gray-backed, Sooty, Noddy, and White Terns. Pelagic waters provide essential foraging sites for numerous shearwaters, petrels, terns, and other seabirds.

www.ingramcontent.com/pod-product-compliance
Lightning Source LLC
Chambersburg PA
CBHW080626290526
45790CB00007B/2949